LOCO SPOTTER'S GUIDE

OSPREY
PUBLISHING

LOCO SPOTTER'S GUIDE

Compiled and Illustrated by Stuart Black

First published in Great Britain in 2017 by Osprey Publishing, PO Box 883, Oxford, OX1 9PL, UK 1385 Broadway, 5th Floor, New York, NY 10018, USA

E-mail: info@ospreypublishing.com

Osprey Publishing, part of Bloomsbury Publishing Plc

> **Editor's Note:**
>
> The locomotives in this book are shown at different scales in order that each example can be seen in as much detail as possible. Their comparative sizes are evident from the lengths given in the specifications tables.

A CIP catalogue record for this book is available from the British Library.

Stuart Black has asserted his right under the Copyright, Designs and Patents Act, 1988, to be identified as the compiler, illustrator and editor of this Work.

All artwork by Stuart Black

ISBN: 978 1 4728 2048 8
PDF ISBN: 978 1 4728 2049 5
ePub ISBN: 978 1 4728 2050 1

Typeset in Conduit and Cambria

Originated by PDQ Digital Media Solutions

Printed in China through World Print Ltd.

17 18 19 20 21   10 9 8 7 6 5 4 3 2 1

Osprey Publishing supports the Woodland Trust, the UK's leading woodland conservation charity. Between 2014 and 2018 our donations will be spent on their Centenary Woods project in the UK.

www.ospreypublishing.com

CONTENTS

INTRODUCTION

The first person to be recognised as a loco spotter was fourteen-year-old Fanny Johnson, who is known to have kept a record of locomotive numbers and names in 1861. However, it was not until the early 1940s that loco spotting took off in earnest when Ian Allan, a young man employed as a public relations clerk by the Southern Railway, set up the Locospotters Club and published a series of books called ABCs. At one point, the Locospotters Club had over 300,000 members. The ABCs were small, pocket-sized books that contained the numbers of all the locomotives operated by British Railways. They were available in individual parts that covered a particular railway region, or as a combined volume. These were supplemented by another book containing locomotive shed allocations. ABCs allowed the loco spotter to tick off the locomotives that he (or she) had seen (or 'copped' as it was known). They generated comradery and rivalry among spotters of all ages in their battles to complete a class or to 'cop' an unusual loco. The hobby reached its peak in the 1950s to 1960s and, despite a diminishing railway, has survived to the present day, albeit to a much lesser degree.

Loco spotting has many different aspects, which range from collecting numbers to the pursuits of the dedicated spotters who participate in 'cabbing', 'shed bashing', and 'haulage bashing'. The latter is perhaps the ultimate as it involves travelling behind as many different locomotives as possible – a time-consuming and expensive pastime! Photography is an important component of the hobby and became increasingly popular with advances in camera technology and image processing. Photographs often hold an important clue towards pinning a date to a picture because the liveries of locomotives are often changed during the course of their lives. Some spotters travel huge distances to chase down elusive locos or to venture into unknown territory, where previously unseen locomotive classes can be found. It is an all-consuming passion that is limited only by the spotter's finances and ability to travel.

But what is the fascination of loco spotting? It is more than just collecting numbers. Locomotives can have interesting names, there are livery variations, different forms and classifications of power, and a life-cycle to follow – new builds, modifications, withdrawals, and fate – was the loco scrapped or one of the lucky few that were preserved?

My own association with this pastime began when I was a mere four years of age. My great-grandfather lived in Aberdeen and his influence as an engine driver filtered down to my father, who in turn passed it on to me. My first school, Poppleton Road Primary, was alongside the main line at York – not far from the huge loco shed and roundhouse that is now the home of the National Railway Museum. So it is not surprising that at such an early age, the sight and sound of steam engines pounding up and down the East Coast Main Line became a fascination. It wasn't long before a trip to the loco shed or a few hours spent on the end of a platform at York station became a regular weekend event.

Those experiences had a huge impact on me as a young lad. I was quickly absorbed by the intrigue of such mighty machines, their numbers and their names. I have no doubt that there was an incidental education process going on too, because my knowledge of obscure things like the names of famous racehorses, breeds of duck, and species of antelopes, to name but a few, was second to none, all because I knew them from the lists of locomotives in my ABCs. Many years on I can still impress family members by answering questions correctly on these subjects during TV quiz shows!

Loco spotting lost its appeal for me after steam locomotives were withdrawn, but the preservation scene and railway modelling have helped to keep the spark alive. I started drawing and painting locomotives when I was in my teens. There was an inner desire to capture the elegance and technical marvel that certain locomotives had impressed upon me. Over subsequent years, I progressed from painting locomotives that I had known and admired to others that had made an impact in their own way.

This book portrays a collection of some of those artworks, and provides a broad sample of the locomotive designs that have graced British rails for over two hundred years. It is hoped that they, and the accompanying text, will help explain to the reader why they have given the loco spotter so much drive, intrigue, and pleasure.

Stuart Black

LIVERIES

The history of liveries on Britain's railways is a complex subject that deserves a book in its own right. The purpose of this small section is to provide the reader with a little knowledge of the subject when relating to the locomotives that are featured in this book. There are numerous books and websites on the subject for those who want to explore the subject in more detail.

A livery portrays the corporate image of the railway company – a selection of colours often accompanied by stylised lettering, lining, and numbering, and crests or coats of arms. A distinctive font can also form part of the identity. For example, the Gill Sans font was introduced by the London & North Eastern Railway in the early 1930s, and was later adopted by British Railways. This was superseded by Rail Alphabet, a typeface designed specifically for British Railways during their rebranding in the late 1960s. Colours are generally picked for their conspicuity (or lack of, for example Wartime Black) and their ability to remain looking clean – a difficult requirement for a steam locomotive!

Before 1923 there was a multitude of different railway companies with extremely colourful liveries, and the absence of colour photography during this period can make research into particular liveries problematical. Between 1923 and 1947 there were only four major railway companies (known

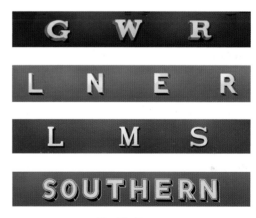

The Big Four

as the 'Big Four') and this reduced the number of different liveries considerably. This era included prestige trains such as the *Coronation* and the *Silver Jubilee*, which introduced striking liveries for both their locomotives and coaches.

The Big Four were united under the umbrella of British Railways after nationalisation on 1 January 1948. This reduced the number of liveries even further and, after a number of experimental liveries were trialled, the Railway Executive settled for simple uniformity, with express passenger and other main line steam locomotives being painted dark green, and all other engines being painted black. Lining was applied in most cases, except on shunting and freight locomotives, which provided a less austere look.

British Railways crests, 1950–56 (left), 1956–65 (right)

Diesel locomotives were generally painted dark green, but there were a few exceptions, and 25 kVa AC electric locomotives were painted in a colour known as Electric Blue.

The situation remained unchanged until the mid-1960s, when a radical new look heralded the end of the steam era. The introduction of a plain blue livery (known as Rail Blue) on locomotives, and a blue and grey livery for passenger coaches, marked the beginning of a modern image under the brand name of British Rail and the iconic double-arrow symbol. A little later, the Total Operations Processing System (TOPS) was adopted. TOPS is a computer system for managing locomotives and rolling stock that is still in use. In the mid-1980s a new InterCity livery (dark grey and beige with red and white bands) was introduced, along with a number of regional colour schemes such as Network South East, and ScotRail. Around this time, special liveries were also introduced for Railfreight locomotives. Initially, this was a drab-looking plain grey with a red stripe, but evolved into a striking, triple-grey scheme, embellished with colourful, freight sub-sector symbols and cast depot plaques. Specific liveries were also introduced for the Civil Engineer's department and the Parcels Sector.

In 1994 British Rail was privatised, which resulted in an explosion of new liveries, and marked the beginning of another new era. Since then there have been approximately two hundred different liveries but some of these have been short-lived due to franchising or the amalgamation of companies. Those that have prevailed include the passenger services served by the FirstGroup, Virgin Trains, Arriva Trains Wales, Arriva CrossCountry, Chiltern Railways, East Midland Trains, Abellio ScotRail and Abellio Greater Anglia. In parallel, full privatisation of freight operations saw the emergence of the English Welsh & Scottish Railway (subsequently purchased by DB Schenker), Freightliner, Direct Rail Services, and GB Railfreight.

Examples of Railway company logos from the privatised era

There are a number of smaller companies who also have access to the British railway network, and together they bring a splash of colour and a variety of liveries not seen since the early twentieth century. In stark contrast to those early days, modern locomotive liveries may also include intricate graphics applied on vinyl, website addresses, advertising, and sponsorship – all a sign of the times!

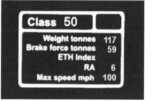

British Rail double-arrow symbol and TOPS data panel

PUFFING BILLY

SPECIFICATIONS

Power Type: Steam
Built: 1813
Withdrawn: 1862
Designer: William Hedley
Builder: Hedley, Forster, and Hackworth
Weight: 8.25 tons
Operator: Wylam Colliery, Northumberland
Preserved: Science Museum, London; replicas at Beamish and Munich

PUFFING BILLY is the world's oldest surviving steam locomotive. It was built in 1813 by William Hedley, Jonathan Forster, and Timothy Hackworth to replace horses on the Wylam Colliery to Lemington-on-Tyne waggonway in Northumberland. Its success was pivotal in promoting the use of steam locomotives as a method of hauling coal at other collieries, and in the development of mechanical transportation in general. Puffing Billy incorporated a number of novel features such as vertical cylinders, and piston rods that extended upwards to pivoted beams. These were connected by rods to a crankshaft beneath the frames, from which gears drove and coupled the wheels. The locomotive remained in service until 1862, when it was lent, and later sold, to the Science Museum in London, where it remains on display. Two similar locomotives were built, and one, named Wylam Dilly, which continued to operate until the early 1880s, can be seen in the Royal Museum, Edinburgh. There is a working replica at the Beamish Museum, and another replica is in the Transport Museum, Munich.

LOCOMOTION

SPECIFICATIONS

Power Type: Steam
Built: 1825
Withdrawn: 1841 (static use until 1857)
Designer: Robert Stephenson
Builder: Robert Stephenson & Co.
Weight: 6.5 tons
Operator: Stockton & Darlington Railway
Preserved: Darlington Railway Centre

LOCOMOTION was the first steam locomotive to haul a passenger train on a public railway. The engine was driven by its designer, George Stephenson, and ran on the Stockton and Darlington Railway on 27 September 1825. It was originally called *Active*, and was the first locomotive to use coupling rods rather than gears to connect its wheels.

On 1 July 1828, *Locomotion*'s boiler exploded at Aycliffe Lane, killing the driver and maiming the water pumper. The engine was rebuilt but as locomotive development was advancing rapidly at the time, it soon became obsolete. After being withdrawn from service in 1841, *Locomotion* was used as a pumping engine until 1857. It was then put on public display and steamed on special occasions, including the Golden Jubilee of the Stockton and Darlington Railway in 1875, and the Stephenson Centenary in 1881. Between 1892 and 1975 it was on display at Darlington station. Following its success, a number of similar locomotives were built, but it is the only one to have survived.

ROCKET

SPECIFICATIONS

Power Type: Steam
Built/Withdrawn: 1829/1844
Designer/Builder: Robert Stephenson
Length: 11 ft
Weight: 4.15 tons
Operator: Liverpool & Manchester Railway
Preserved: Original at Science Museum, London; replica at National Railway Museum, York

ROCKET was a prototype locomotive built for the Liverpool & Manchester Railway's Rainhill Trials – a competition with a £500 prize that was held in 1829 to determine the best form of power for the railway. Up until this time, locomotives had been designed for use at collieries and for short journeys, so the challenge was to build an engine that was capable of hauling passengers at a reasonable speed between towns and cities. Four other locomotives took part but *Rocket* was the outright winner. In comparison to other designs it was light, fast, and powerful.

The key to *Rocket*'s victory was the bringing together of a number of features to improve steaming – this included the use of a multiple-tube boiler which went on to become standard practice for locomotives throughout the steam era. Following *Rocket*'s success, a number of similar engines were built, and the Liverpool & Manchester Railway became the world's first inter-city railway. *Rocket* was retired in 1834 but spent a further ten years working on a colliery line in Cumberland.

FIRE FLY

SPECIFICATIONS

Power Type: Steam
Built: 1840
Withdrawn: 1870
Designer: Daniel Gooch
Builder: Jones, Turner & Evans (and various others)
Number Built: 62 (plus a replica built in 2005)
Wheel Arrangement: 2-2-2 Broad Gauge (7 ft ¼ in)
Length: 39 ft 4 in
Weight: 24.2 tons
Operator: Great Western Railway
Preserved: Replica at Didcot Railway Centre

In the early years when there was no overall plan for the development of the railways, different gauges of track were being used. Between London and Bristol, Isambard Kingdom Brunel pioneered a broad gauge (7 ft ¼ in) track for the Great Western Railway. *Fire Fly* was the first of a class of sixty-two locomotives built between 1840 and 1842 for passenger services on that line. Broad gauge allowed much faster speeds than had previously been achieved, and the class gave performances that were the best in the world at the time. On 13 June 1842, one member of the class, *Phlegethon,* hauled the first Royal Train from Slough to London with Queen Victoria on board and in 1845 another class member, *Ixion,* was officially recorded at 61 mph during trials. Broad gauge was abandoned in favour of standard gauge (4 ft 8½ in) in 1892.

An operational replica of *Fire Fly* was built by the Fire Fly Trust, and has operated on a short stretch of broad gauge line at Didcot Railway Centre since 2005.

OLD COPPERNOB

The Furness Railway was an independent railway that was conceived to meet the needs of transporting iron ore and slate from the mines and quarries of the Furness peninsula in Cumbria. The railway was instrumental in the development of the region's iron, steel, and shipbuilding industries.

Old Coppernob was the third of four locomotives built for the first passenger services on the railway. The first two were built in 1844, and the second two were built in 1846. The design became known as the 'Bury Type' after their designer Edward Bury. Many of its features – such as inside horizontal cylinders and wrought-iron frames – underpinned future locomotive designs. It had a much cleaner and modern look than previous designs, although without a cab the footplate crew were still fully exposed to the elements. The nickname *Old Coppernob* originates from the prominent dome-shaped copper firebox. The locomotives were built in Liverpool, and delivered by boat to Piel Island on the southern tip of the Furness peninsula.

No. 3 hauled the first passenger train on the railway on 24 August 1846, and is the only survivor of the class. As newer and faster locomotives were introduced, these venerable machines were relegated to freight duties, hauling iron ore and slate between the mines, the ironworks, the steelworks, and the docks. *Old Coppernob*'s last operational days were spent as a shunter at Barrow docks, where it continued to give service until December 1898, by which time it was the oldest operational locomotive in the country.

Following withdrawal from service, it went on display in a large glass case at Barrow Central station. However, during the Blitz in 1941, a German bomb fell on the station, and scars from the shrapnel can still be seen on the locomotive today. Following this, it was put into store but was later moved to the British Museum of Transport, London. In 1975 it was moved to York, and is now part of the National Collection. It was returned to steam in 1996 to take part in the celebrations for the 150th anniversary of the Furness Railway.

Old Coppernob

SPECIFICATIONS

Power Type: Steam
Built: 1846
Withdrawn: 1898
Designer: Edward Bury

Builders: Bury, Curtis & Kennedy
Wheel Arrangement: 0-4-0
Length: 37 ft 3 in
Weight: 19.5 tons
Livery: Furness Railway (Indian Red with Black Lining)
Preserved: National Railway Museum, York

STIRLING SINGLE

Technological advances, competition, and the widespread expansion of railway lines led to a rapid development of locomotive designs in the second half of the nineteenth century. In the 1860s, some designers believed that large driving wheels were necessary to achieve high speeds through better adhesion. Patrick Stirling was such a man, and he produced one of the most striking and elegant locomotive types to emerge in this period. It was the Great Northern Railway Class G – designed for the high-speed express services between London and York – which included the 'Flying Scotsman'. Due to their prominent 8-foot driving wheels they became affectionately known as the 'Stirling Singles', and had the power to haul up to twenty-six carriages at high average speeds. They were also nicknamed 'Eight-footers', and were the fastest locomotives in the country at the time.

Thirty-seven Class Gs were built between 1870 and 1883. These were followed by sixteen similar locomotives (Class G1 and G2), with the last ten having larger boilers and pistons.

In 1888, there was an unofficial Race to the North between the rival east and west coast railway companies. Stirling Singles excelled and recorded top speeds of up to 85 mph, with average speeds of 58 mph between London and York. The Stirling Singles had long and successful lives, but the introduction of larger and heavier coaches from 1895 put too much demand on them, and they were replaced on express duties by more modern designs.

No. 1 was withdrawn from service in 1907 (although other members of the class survived until 1916), and it was retained for preservation, originally in the old Railway Museum, York, and later in the National Railway Museum. In 1938, it was returned to steam to haul a special train to mark the fiftieth anniversary of the Race to the North, and for an excursion from London to Cambridge for railway enthusiasts. In 1975, the locomotive took part in the Rail 150 Cavalcade of Steam at Shildon, and spent almost a year operating on the Great Central Railway in the early 1980s.

No. 1

SPECIFICATIONS

Class: G
Power Type: Steam
First Built: 1870
Withdrawn: 1907–16
Designer: Patrick Stirling
Builder: Doncaster Works

Number Built: 37 (plus 16 Class G1 and G2)
Wheel Arrangement: 4-2-2
Length: 50 ft 2 in
Weight: 65 tons
Max Speed: 85 mph
Livery: GNR Apple Green
Preserved: 1 at National Railway Museum, Shildon

STROUDLEY CLASS A1 'TERRIER'

The Stroudley Class A1 tank locomotives hold a unique place in British locomotive history, due to their persistence and longevity. They were introduced in 1872, and played a key role in the drive towards standardisation. Although considered obsolete at the turn of the nineteenth century, many soldiered on and several were still operating in the early 1960s.

Designed by William Stroudley, these diminutive but powerful tank locomotives were built to meet the needs of the London Brighton & South Coast Railway. A total of fifty were constructed at Brighton Works between 1872 and 1880. The locomotives acquired the nickname 'Terrier' due to the bark of their exhaust. Initially the class were employed on frequent, short-distance commuter services. Some were used on the East London Line and travelled under the River Thames via the Thames Tunnel. The expansion of the commuter belt to towns such as Croydon can be attributed largely to the Terriers, as their speed allowed people to work further from the centre of London. They were such reliable and versatile performers that when commuter trains became heavier and they were displaced from these duties, the class found useful employment on branch lines and on shunting duties. When withdrawn by the LBSCR, many of the class were sold to other railway companies (including four to the Isle of Wight Railway), and a few were put to use at locomotive and carriage works.

Twenty-two members of the class were rebuilt between 1911 and 1943 with new boilers, extended smoke boxes, and other refinements. These were known as Class A1X. In 1960, No. 32655 (formerly No. 55 *Stepney*) was purchased from British Railways, and became the first steam locomotive to enter service on a standard gauge preserved line in Great Britain. The last scheduled passenger services for the class on British Railways was on the Hayling Island Branch, which continued to use Terriers until November 1963. One of those engines, No. 32636 (formerly No. 72 *Fenchurch*), had the distinction of being the oldest operational locomotive on British Railways, at ninety-one years of age.

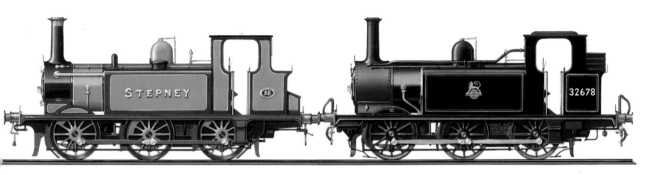

55 *Stepney* and 32678 (Class A1 and A1X)

SPECIFICATIONS

Class: A1 and A1X
Power Type: Steam
First Built: 1872
Withdrawn: 1901–63
Designer: William Stroudley
Builder: Brighton Works

Number Built: 50 (includes 22 A1X)
Wheel Arrangement: 0-6-0
Length: 26 ft ½ in
Weight: 27.5 tons (A1), 28.25 tons (A1X)
Max Speed: 60 mph
Livery: LBSCR
Preserved: 10 (includes 1 at National Railway Museum, York, and 1 in Canada)

CALEDONIAN SINGLE

The Caledonian Railway was a major Scottish railway company that was formed to connect the railways of Scotland and England. Its development was rapid, and from 15 February 1848 it became possible to travel on a continuous line between London and Glasgow. A network of branch and commuter lines soon emerged from the principal routes.

The *Caledonian Single* was an engine that had a stroke of remarkably good fortune. It was built with the sole purpose of being the Caledonian Railway's star exhibit at the Edinburgh International Exhibition in 1886. It featured a single, large driving wheel, similar to that of the Stirling Single, but this wheel arrangement was never adopted by the Caledonian Railway, and the locomotive remained unique. After entering service, the locomotive was found to give excellent performances, particularly on routes with steep gradients. During the unofficial Race to the North in 1888, it was charged with taking the west coast train forward from Carlisle to Edinburgh – a journey of 101 miles – which it covered comfortably in a little over 100 minutes.

Also known as *Caley 123*, this unique and famous engine went on to give several years of useful service on routine passenger routes between Edinburgh, Carlisle, and Glasgow, before being relegated to more sedate duties. As such it was notable for being given the honour of Royal Train Pilot during the reign of three monarchs: Queen Victoria, King Edward VII and King George V. In 1923, when the Caledonian Railway became absorbed in the London Midland & Scottish Railway, the locomotive was painted Midland Red and given the number 14010.

Retirement came in 1935, by which time the locomotive had gained the distinction of being the last single-driving-wheel express locomotive to run in Great Britain. It was an obvious candidate for preservation, and was initially stored at St Rollox, Glasgow. In 1958, the locomotive was returned to operational condition, and hauled several special trains and rail tours before being retired as a museum exhibit in 1965.

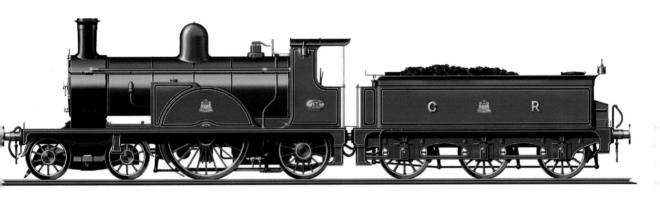

Caley 123

SPECIFICATIONS

Class: Caledonian Single
Power Type: Steam
Built: 1886
Withdrawn: 1935
Designer: Dugald Drummond
Builder: Neilson & Co., Springburn Works

Number Built: 1
Wheel Arrangement: 4-2-2
Max Speed: 60 mph
Length: 49 ft 2¼ in
Weight: 41.35 tons
Liveries: CR Blue, Midland Red
Preserved: Riverside Museum, Glasgow

DEAN SINGLE

The Great Western Railway was still using broad gauge track when its Chief Mechanical Engineer, William Dean, introduced his new express passenger locomotives in 1891. However, plans were already in place to adopt the standard gauge, so his locomotives were built initially as 'convertibles' with a 2-2-2 wheel arrangement. The first eight of the class had this unusual feature, which required the wheels to be on the outside of the frames. As was common practice at the time, the design featured a large (7 ft 8½ in) single driving wheel, and they became known as the Dean Singles. They were converted to standard gauge in 1892, by shortening the axles and placing the wheels inside the frames.

The next twenty-two locomotives were built as standard gauge from new, but the modified arrangement made the weight of the locomotives unbalanced, and they were unsteady at speed. A major modification followed, which lengthened the frames and introduced a leading bogie to allow a 4-2-2 wheel arrangement. This transformation gave the class a more elegant and graceful appearance. A further fifty locomotives were built to this specification between 1894 and 1899, bringing the total number in the class to eighty. They were also known as the GWR 3031 Class (after the first locomotive to be built), and the Achilles Class.

The class was the mainstay of traction for the London to the West of England expresses during the first decade of the twentieth century. Despite a number of modifications and improvements during their lives, they were eventually ousted by more powerful classes, and were put in charge of the less-demanding services between London, Birmingham, and Wolverhampton.

Two Dean Singles were selected for Royal Train duties during Queen Victoria's Jubilee celebrations in 1897, and one, No. 3041, was specially renamed *The Queen*. A full-size, non-working replica of this locomotive was built in 1982 for a Railways and Royalty exhibition, and is now on display at Windsor station, albeit without a tender.

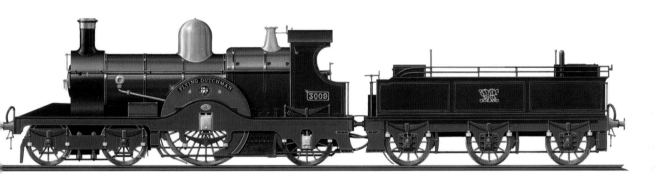

3009 *Flying Dutchman*

SPECIFICATIONS

Class: GWR 3031
Power Type: Steam
First Built: 1892
Withdrawn: 1908–16
Designer: William Dean
Builder: Swindon Works

Number Built: 80
Wheel Arrangement: 4-2-2
Weight: 76.7 tons
Max Speed: 85 mph
Livery: GWR
Preserved: 0 (one non-working replica, Windsor)

ARMSTRONG CLASS

The Great Western Railway produced some of the most elegant steam locomotives of all time, and their appearance was further enhanced by eye-catching liveries. Following on from the graceful Dean Singles came another masterpiece of late-nineteenth-century engineering, in the form of the Armstrong Class. Only four were built, and they were all rebuilds of older designs (three were originally broad gauge locomotives). They represented an important advance in locomotive design, as they set the bench mark for a range of 4-4-0 inside cylinder locomotives that were introduced in the following years. The Armstrongs were coupled to the same type of tender as those attached to the Dean Singles, which incorporated a simple type of condensing apparatus to return water to the tank, while also providing a method of preheating the water.

The four locomotives kept their original numbers (7, 8, 14, and 16) and were named after prominent figures in the GWR – *Armstrong*, *Gooch*, *Charles Saunders*, and *Brunel*. Initially they were put to work on the London to Bristol line alongside the Dean Singles, but from around 1910 they were moved to Wolverhampton to work the express services that ran north from there. Between 1905 and 1911, all four locomotives were rebuilt extensively, with new boilers and fireboxes. They were rebuilt again in 1915, this time with smaller driving wheels, and a larger, tapered boiler. Following this modification, the four locomotives were incorporated into the GWR 4100 Class, and were renumbered 4169 to 4172, to conform to the GWR locomotive numbering system that was evolving at the time.

By the end of their working lives, very little of the original components of these engines remained. They were all withdrawn between 1928 and 1930, their place being succeeded by more powerful 4-6-0 designs such as the Castle Class. Sadly, despite their complex histories and significant role in locomotive development, none of these graceful and purposeful machines were preserved, and all four were scrapped.

16 *Brunel*

SPECIFICATIONS

Class: Armstrong
Power Type: Steam
First Built: 1894
Withdrawn: 1928–30
Designer: William Dean
Builder: Swindon Works

Number Built: 4
Wheel Arrangement: 4-4-0
Weight: 87.55 tons
Livery: GWR
Names: Prominent GWR figures: *7 Armstrong*, *8 Gooch*, *14 Charles Saunders*, *16 Brunel*
Preserved: 0

DRUMMOND T9 CLASS

By the end of the nineteenth century, the 4-4-0 wheel arrangement that had been pioneered by the designers of the Great Western Railway had become widely adopted for express locomotive designs by other railway companies. The London & South Western Railway was no exception, but their initial design was not powerful enough to cope with the increasing weight of passenger trains. Dugald Drummond, a Scottish railway engineer who had taken up an appointment with the LSWR in 1895, was instrumental in their development, and his most successful design emerged in 1899. It was known as the T9 Class, and the power and speed of these locomotives soon earned them the nickname 'Greyhounds'.

An initial order for sixty-five locomotives was placed and an additional member of the class was built for display at the Glasgow Exhibition in 1901. Building took place at both the LSWR Works at Nine Elms, London, and at the Dubs & Co. Works, Glasgow. Initially the T9s were delivered with six-wheeled tenders that could carry 4 tons of coal and 3,500 gallons of water. However, on some routes this allowed very little surplus of water, so a new eight-wheeled tender (known as a 'water cart'), capable of carrying 4,000 gallons was introduced. With this tender, the T9s could cover all the key routes from London to destinations in the south west, including Portsmouth and Exeter. Engines fitted with the smaller six-wheel tender still found useful employment on express services to the Kent and Sussex coasts.

During the course of their long and successful lives, the T9s received a number of improvements, including the fitting of superheaters. Some locomotives also received a replacement chimney (known as a stove pipe), which was shorter than the original and allowed the class to run on lines that had a lower loading gauge. In 1947, thirteen T9s were converted to oil burning, but this unsuccessful experiment led to their early demise. The majority of the class were withdrawn in the 1950s, but a few remained operational in the early 1960s.

122

SPECIFICATIONS

Class: T9

Power Type: Steam

First Built: 1899

Withdrawn: 1948–63

Designer: Dugald Drummond

Builder: LSWR Nine Elms Works (35); Dubs & Co., Glasgow (31)

Number Built: 66

Wheel Arrangement: 4-4-0

Length: 63 ft 9 in

Weight: 49.6 tons (with eight-wheel tender)

Livery: LSWR and SR (various shades of green, black) BR (Lined Black)

Preserved: 1 (No. 120 at National Railway Museum, on loan to the Swanage Railway)

MIDLAND COMPOUND

A compound steam engine is one in which steam is expanded to improve the efficiency of the fuel and water. The steam is used more than once, first in a high-pressure cylinder and then in lower-pressure cylinders. Invented in 1781, this type of engine was used extensively in textile mills and ships but it was not until the latter part of the nineteenth century that they found favour in British locomotive designs. An engineer named Francis Webb produced a number of compound locomotives for the London and North Western Railway, the first entering service in 1882. The North Eastern Railway also employed compound locomotive designs in the 1890s. However, it was the Midland Railway that, in 1902, introduced two prototype compound locomotives that were to underpin the most successful British compound design of all. These were designed by Samuel Johnson and were heavily based on the NER design. They were an immediate success, acquitting themselves well on the demanding route between Leeds and Carlisle. The following year, three similar locomotives were built, and these were put to work on services between London, Nottingham, Leicester, and Derby. Appropriately, they became known as the Midland Compounds.

Johnson's successor, Richard Deeley, made improvements that simplified the original design and incorporated a larger firebox. Forty locomotives were built to this specification between 1905 and 1909. In 1913, a superheated boiler was fitted to one of these engines, and this offered further efficiencies. As a consequence, all members of the class were similarly modified. On formation of the London Midland & Scottish Railway in 1923, the Midland Compound was adopted as a standard express locomotive and a further 190 were built between 1924 and 1927. Despite an early decline in enthusiasm for the compound steam locomotive, the introduction of superheaters ensured that the Midland Compounds remained in widespread service across the LMS, and later BR, until their withdrawal in the 1950s.

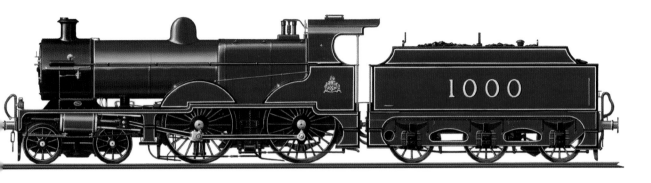

1000

SPECIFICATIONS

Class: Midland Compound
Power Type: Steam
First Built: 1902
Withdrawn: 1951–61
Number Built: 240
Designer: Samuel Johnson

Builders: Derby Works (120), Horwich Works (20), Vulcan Foundry (75), NBL Co. (25)
Wheel Arrangement: 4-4-0
Length: 56 ft 8 in
Weight: 104.3 tons
Livery: MR and LMS (both Crimson Lake), LMS (Black), BR (Black, Lined Black)
Preserved: 1 – National Railway Museum

CITY CLASS

During the latter half of the nineteenth century, the Great Western Railway built some very successful engines with single driving wheels, but they struggled to cope with the demands of increasingly heavier passenger trains. Designers therefore turned to 4-4-0 designs, and some of these were modified in attempts to improve performance. This included the Atbara Class, which evolved into the City Class. Their most notable feature was a mix of traditional design – double frames and inside cylinders – with a modern tapered boiler and large firebox. Building of the first ten locomotives began at Swindon in 1903, and they were joined by ten converted Atbara Class locomotives between 1907 and 1909. They were also known as 3700 Class, and worked predominately on the express routes between Plymouth and London.

These fine engines marked an important point in British locomotive development, as they were the foundation of the designs that would dominate the twentieth century. From around 1910, superheaters were fitted, which gave improved performance, but despite their success and popularity, the City Class was quickly overshadowed by the GWR's emerging powerful 4-6-0 express locomotives.

One member of the class, No. 3440 *City of Truro*, the two-thousandth locomotive built at Swindon Works, is claimed to have attained an unofficial speed in excess of 100 mph. It was recorded on a stopwatch by railway journalist Charles Rous-Marten, while travelling on the Bristol to Plymouth Ocean Mails train on 9 May 1904. The claim has been subject to much controversy, but it enabled the locomotive to acquire lasting fame, and it was preserved as a result. In preservation, *City of Truro* has led an active life. It was withdrawn in 1931 but was brought out of retirement in 1951 for regular service on BR's Western Region between Didcot and Southampton. In 1961 it was withdrawn once again and displayed in the GWR museum, Swindon. The locomotive was given further reprieves in 1984 and 2004, when it enjoyed long spells of running on the main line and at heritage railways.

3440 *City of Truro*

SPECIFICATIONS

Class: City
Power Type: Steam
First Built: 1902
Withdrawn: 1927–31
Designer: George Jackson Churchward
Builder: Swindon Works

Number Built: 20 (includes 10 converted from Atbara class)
Wheel Arrangement: 4-4-0
Weight: 92.1 tons
Max Speed: 100 mph +
Livery: GWR (various)
Preserved: 1 – National Collection

NBR K CLASS

The North British Railway was opened in 1846, and controlled the lines in much of eastern and southern Scotland. It developed more by a process of amalgamation among existing companies than that of expansion. Its network was centred on Edinburgh, and had routes into England via Berwick-upon-Tweed and Carlisle, which led to intense rivalry with the Caledonian Railway. In 1890, the opening of the Forth Bridge allowed through-services to Dundee and Aberdeen, giving the NBR a significant advantage.

William Reid, who began his career as an apprentice at the NBR Works in 1879, gained considerable experience of locomotive development, and became Locomotive Superintendent between 1903 and 1919. He designed a number of locomotives, and the K Class was the final development of his 4-4-0 mixed-traffic types. They were based on his earlier J Class, and were built at the NBR's Cowlairs Works over a seven-year period. They had superheated boilers, and were named after Scottish glens, which earned them the nickname, the 'Glens'.

The class saw extensive use on the West Highland Line (Glasgow to Fort William and Mallaig), which had been acquired by the NBR in 1908. Here they coped admirably on the steeply graded and twisting track, although double heading was often required on heavier trains. Eventually they were deployed all over the NBR network, and put in some fine performances on express services between Edinburgh, Glasgow, and Dundee. In addition, they were a common sight on excursions, football specials and troop trains.

When the NBR became a constituent of the LNER in 1923, the class became known as D34. Gradually they were succeeded by the more modern and powerful Gresley and Thompson locomotives. Withdrawals began as early as 1946, but the majority of the class survived until the late 1950s, and the last five were withdrawn in 1961. One example has been preserved, No. 256 *Glen Douglas*. It was restored and kept in working order until 1965, before taking up residence in the Glasgow Museum of Transport (now Riverside Museum).

256 Glen Douglas

SPECIFICATIONS

Class: NBR K (LNER D34)
Power Type: Steam
First Built: 1913
Withdrawn: 1946–61
Designer: William Reid
Builder: NBR Cowlairs Works

Number Built: 32
Wheel Arrangement: 4-4-0
Length: 56 ft 3 in
Weight: 103.85 tons (full)
Livery: NBR (Green), LNER (Apple Green, Black), BR (Black)
Preserved: 1 at Riverside Museum, Glasgow

KING ARTHUR CLASS

Many British locomotive classes evolved through improvements to existing designs. The Class N15 was a classic example of this philosophy, and it had a complex history. It was based on a successful and robust mixed-traffic locomotive, known as the Class H15, which had been introduced by Robert Urie in 1913 for the London & South Western Railway. Urie developed this design into an express passenger locomotive in 1916, but due to the manufacturing demands of World War I, building did not commence until 1918. The N15 was a bigger engine all round with 6 ft 7 in driving wheels, larger cylinders, and a tapered boiler. It was coupled to an eight-wheeled tender that had a capacity of 5,000 gallons of water and 5 tons of coal, which gave considerable range. Twenty of these impressive looking machines were built for use on the LSWR's express services, and all were absorbed into the Southern Railway in 1923.

However, the N15s struggled on the more demanding routes, so the SR's Chief Mechanical Engineer, Richard Maunsell, modified them by providing more efficient draughting, and a better steaming capability. Due to a shortage of express motive power, the SR ordered a further fifty-four locomotives of the improved design. These were built in three batches between 1925 and 1927. The first batch included conversions from previous classes, the second batch was built by the North British Locomotive Company in Glasgow, and the third batch was built at the SR's Eastleigh Works. For publicity purposes, they were named after characters from the legend of King Arthur and the Knights of the Round Table. They became known as the King Arthur Class and, depending on their origin, they were nicknamed the 'Urie Arthurs', the 'Scotch Arthurs', and the 'Eastleigh Arthurs'. In 1926 they became the first British locomotive class to be fitted with smoke deflectors.

The King Arthurs were dependable locomotives that gained praise for their excellent acceleration and high speed. They were the mainstay of power for express services on the SR until demoted to secondary duties by the introduction of the Bulleid Pacifics in the late 1940s.

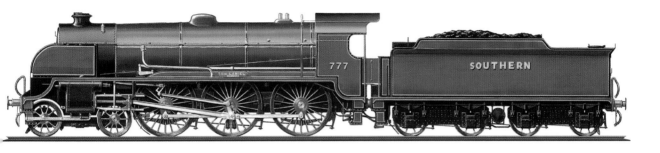

777 Sir Lamiel

SPECIFICATIONS

Class: N15 (King Arthur)
Power Type: Steam
First Built: 1918
Withdrawn: 1953–62
Designers: R. W. Urie and R. E. L. Maunsell
Builders: Eastleigh Works & NBL Co.

Number Built: 74
Wheel Arrangement: 4-6-0
Length: 66 ft 5¼ in
Weight: 137.2 tons
Liveries: SR ('Urie' Green, 'Maunsell' Green, Wartime Black), BR (Lined Green)
Names: Characters from the legend of King Arthur
Preserved: 1 – National Collection, loaned to heritage lines

IMPROVED DIRECTOR CLASS

In 1899, the Great Central Railway was the last of the major railway companies to reach London (Marylebone). As its name implied, the GCR's main lines were sandwiched between the other major routes to the east and west of the country, and its principal destinations were Nottingham, Manchester, and Sheffield. In places, it had long, demanding gradients, which meant that trains had to run with light loadings. The company's Locomotive Superintendent, John G. Robinson, recognised the need for more powerful express locomotives, and one of his more successful designs was the Class 11E. These were introduced in 1913, and became known as the Director Class, but only ten were built before the onset of World War I. By the time building recommenced in 1919, a number of enhancements had been made to the design, which included improved piston valves and a modern cab. These differences led to the new locomotives being classified 11F, and they adopted the name Improved Director. Upon the grouping of the Big Four in 1923, the London & North Eastern Railway inherited the class, and saw them as ideal engines to fulfil their requirement for express passenger locomotives on the former North British Railway lines. A further batch of twenty-four locomotives was built in 1924, but these engines had lower cabs, chimneys, and boiler mountings to allow them to travel on more restrictive lines. The LNER classified these engines D11/2, the former GCR locomotives becoming Class D11/1. Such was the popularity of the class that they were used on some Pullman services between 1927 and 1932.

Although a distinctly old-fashioned design, the Improved Directors continued to find work in the Midlands and Scotland up until the 1950s. The introduction of the Thompson Class B1s eventually displaced them, but many spent considerable time in storage being held in reserve. Withdrawals commenced at the end of 1958, and the last was taken out of service at Edinburgh Haymarket shed in early 1962. Only one escaped scrapping – No. 506 *Butler Henderson*, the first Class 11F to be built. It is the only surviving GCR express passenger locomotive.

506 *Butler Henderson*

SPECIFICATIONS

Class: GCR 11F, LNER D11/1, D11/2
Power Type: Steam
First Built: 1919
Withdrawn: 1958–62
Designer: John G. Robinson
Builder: GCR Gorton Works (and others)
Number Built: 35 (GCR 11, LNER 24)

Wheel Arrangement: 4-4-0
Length: 58 ft 11½ in
Weight: 109.45 tons
Liveries: GCR (Green & Red), LNER (Apple Green, Lined Black), BR (Black, Lined Black)
Names: Directors of the GCR, WWI battles, royalty, characters from Walter Scott literature
Preserved: 1 – National Collection, loaned to heritage lines

GNSR CLASS F

The Great North of Scotland Railway covered the north east of Scotland and was opened in 1854. From Aberdeen it went to Elgin, Fraserburgh, and Ballater, and had a network of branch lines. Its locomotive construction and repair works was based at Inverurie, but only two classes were built there – Class V and Class F. The Class V had been introduced by William Pickersgill in 1899, and when the GNSR needed to replace some of its ageing locomotive fleet after World War I, Pickersgill's successor, Thomas Heywood, introduced a superheated version known as the Class F. It was one of the GNSR's last designs, and eight were built for mixed-traffic duties between 1920 and 1921. Six were built by the North British Locomotive Company in Glasgow, and two were built at the Inverurie Works. They were the best passenger locomotives the GNSR ever owned, and were the only ones to receive names. One member of the class (No. 49) was temporarily fitted with Scarab oil-burning equipment during a coal miners' strike in 1921.

The GNSR became part of the London and North Eastern Railway after the Railway Grouping of 1923. When taken into LNER stock, Class F became Class D40, along with thirteen examples of GNSR's older Class V. A notable duty for the class was double-heading on the Royal Train when conveying royalty to Balmoral Castle via the Deeside line.

Seven members of the class passed into British Railways ownership in 1948, and the last was withdrawn in 1958. By this time, the class had been relegated to secondary duties after the introduction of the LNER Class B12s and Class B1s.

The last operational locomotive, No. 62277 (formerly GNSR No. 49 *Gordon Highlander*), had been allocated to Kittybrewster shed, Aberdeen, throughout most of its working life, but ended its days on the Speyside line. After retirement it was restored to GNSR livery (although not its original Black), and hauled a number of special trains until it was retired to the Glasgow Museum of Transport in 1966. More recently it was moved to the Scottish Railway Museum at Bo'ness.

49 *Gordon Highlander*

SPECIFICATIONS

Class: F
Power Type: Steam
First Built: 1920
Withdrawn: 1947–58
Designer: Thomas Heywood
Builder: NBL Co. (8), Inverurie Works (2)

Number Built: 8
Wheel Arrangement: 4-4-0
Length: 53 ft 1½ in
Weight: 86.05 tons (Full)
Livery: GNSR (Lined Green, Lined Black), LNER (Apple Green, Black), BR (Lined Black)
Preserved: 1 – Scottish Railway Museum

GRESLEY CLASS N2

4750

SPECIFICATIONS

Power Type: Steam
First Built/Withdrawn: 1920/1955–62
Designer: Nigel Gresley
Builders: North British Locomotive Co. (and others)
Number Built: 107
Wheel Arrangement: 0-6-2T
Length: 37 ft 11¾ in
Weight: 70.25 tons
Liveries: GNR (Apple Green), LNER (Black), BR (Lined Black)
Preserved: 1 (No. 4744 [BR No. 69523])

Nigel Gresley designed the Class N2 tank locomotive to meet a motive-power requirement for heavy commuter trains in the post-World-War-I period. The N2 was based on the highly successful Ivatt Class N1 tank locomotive that dated back to 1907. The N2 had larger cylinders and piston valves, greater water capacity, and a superheated boiler. Due to their acceleration and relatively high speed, the class was an immediate success, and they were put to work on Kings Cross suburban services. Members of the class also found their way to Glasgow, Edinburgh, and Dundee to perform similar duties, and some were allocated to sheds in Yorkshire.

A notable feature of some of the London-based N2 tanks was a squat chimney and condensing equipment (as shown), which enabled them to run on underground lines between Kings Cross and Moorgate. The introduction of diesels on suburban services in the late 1950s forced the N2s into redundancy, and all but one were scrapped.

FOWLER CLASS 3F 'JINTY'

7303

SPECIFICATIONS

Power Type: Steam
First Built/Withdrawn: 1924–31/1959–67 (1970 in industrial service)
Designer: Henry Fowler
Builders: NBL Co., Hunslet, Vulcan Foundry, and others
Number Built: 422
Wheel Arrangement: 0-6-0T
Length/Weight: 31 ft 4¾ in/49.5 tons
Max Speed: 60 mph
Operator: LMS, S&DJR, WD, BR, (1 – NCB)
Liveries: LMS (Black), S&DJR (Blue), WD (Black), BR (Black)

W hen the London Midland and Scottish Railway formed in 1923, it adopted the Midland Railway's 1900 Class tank locomotive as a template for a new, standard, shunting locomotive which became known as the Fowler Class 3F. Initially they were nicknamed 'Jockos', but 'Jinty' became more favourable in later years. The design, which dated back to the late 1890s, was given only minor changes, and was built in large quantities by a number of different contractors over an eight-year period. They proved to be reliable and versatile little engines, and soon found their work expanding beyond shunting. Some were equipped with a carriage-heating capability, which allowed them to be employed on local and suburban passenger services. They were widespread across the LMS network, and seven were built exclusively for use on the Somerset & Dorset Joint Railway. Eight members of the class were acquired by the War Department in 1940 and saw service in France. Three were destroyed during hostilities, and the remaining five were repatriated to the LMS.

CASTLE CLASS

When introduced in 1923, the Great Western Railway's Castle Class claimed to be the most powerful express locomotive in Great Britain. This caused much controversy and led to a locomotive exchange in 1925 between the GWR and LNER, in order that a comparison could be made with the larger Gresley A1 Pacifics. The Castles acquitted themselves well and proved to be more powerful and efficient. A similar evaluation took place in 1926 with the LMS, and once again the GWR design outperformed its rivals.

The success of the Castle Class was put down to a design that had evolved from the Star Class. It incorporated four cylinders, a 4-6-0 wheel arrangement with good weight distribution, a tapered boiler, and a Belpaire firebox. Many subsequent classes of steam locomotive were influenced by the Castle Class, including the Gresley A3 Pacifics, the Stanier Black 5s, and some of the British Railways Standard Classes. The Castles gave superb performances over demanding routes, and quickly established themselves on prestigious services. This included the Cheltenham Flyer which, from 1932, was scheduled to cover the 77.3 miles from Swindon to Paddington in just sixty-five minutes, and which required an average speed of over 71 mph – the world's fastest train at the time. Other notable services that the Castles were entrusted with included the Bristolian and the Torbay Express. Such was their versatility that they could be seen just about anywhere on the GWR's main lines, and they were also put in charge of express freight.

During the course of their working lives, the Castles received a number of modifications that further improved their performance. Most notably, the use of larger superheaters and double blast pipes provided a little more power and better steaming with poor coal. The original 3,500-gallon tender was soon replaced by a 4,000-gallon version of which there were two types, one designed by Collett and a flush-sided design introduced in the latter years by Hawksworth. Eight members of the class have survived into preservation, and several of them have ventured back onto the main line.

7033 Hartlebury Castle

SPECIFICATIONS

Class: GWR Castle
Power Type: Steam
First Built: 1923
Withdrawn: 1950–65
Designer: C. B. Collett
Builder: GWR (later BR) Swindon
Number Built: 171 (includes 16 rebuilds)

Wheel Arrangement: 4-6-0
Length: 65 ft 2 in
Weight: 126.55 tons
Max Speed: 100 mph
Liveries: GWR (various), BR (Green)
Names: Most named after castles (also earls, abbeys, WWII aircraft and symbolic GWR names)
Preserved: 8 (1 at Science Museum, London)

LORD NELSON CLASS

The mid-1920s was an important period in British locomotive history when the 'Big Four' companies produced some exceptional locomotives. In particular, their new express passenger designs were large, powerful, and impressive machines. Among these, the Southern Railway had introduced the King Arthur Class, but they could not meet the demands of the heavier expresses that were expected to exceed 500 tons. Richard Maunsell's challenge was to build a more powerful engine than the King Arthur, while keeping the weight down due to the Southern's line restrictions. A skilful and well-balanced design ensured that when the first of his new locomotives took to the rails in 1926, it was the most powerful locomotive in Britain. The first locomotive in the class was named *Lord Nelson*, and it was tested thoroughly for two years before any further were built. The design was unusual in giving eight exhaust beats per revolution instead of the customary four, due to the driving axle cranks being set at 135 degrees instead of the usual 90 degrees, which gave a more even transmission of power. However, they did not live up to expectations due to poor steaming, and it was not until over a decade later that modifications to the blast pipe and chimney enabled their full potential to be realised.

Primary duties for the Lord Nelsons included the continental boat trains between Victoria and Dover, and express services from Waterloo to the south west. The class received a number of modifications during their lives: smoke deflectors were fitted from 1929 and new cylinders were introduced from 1939. One locomotive (No. 859) was given smaller driving wheels and another (No. 860) was given a longer boiler as experiments to improve their performance, but neither offered any significant advantage. Over the course of their lives the locomotives were also coupled to a variety of types of tender including a six-wheel version, but all ended up with high-sided, self-trimming, eight-wheel tenders. Although the introduction of the Bulleid Pacifics in 1941 stole their limelight, the Lord Nelsons continued to give reliable service until their withdrawal in 1961–2.

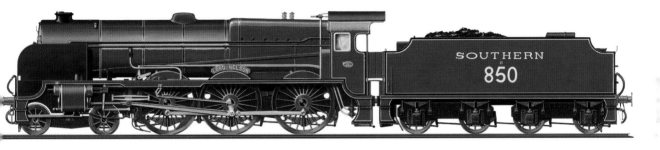

850 *Lord Nelson*

SPECIFICATIONS

Class: Lord Nelson
Power Type: Steam
First Built: 1926
Withdrawn: 1961–2
Designers: R. E. L. Maunsell
Builders: Eastleigh Works

Number Built: 16
Wheel Arrangement: 4-6-0
Length: 69 ft 9¾ in
Weight: 141.45 tons
Liveries: SR (Malachite Green, Olive Green, Wartime Black), BR (Brunswick Green)
Names: Famous British admirals
Preserved: 1 – National Collection, loaned to heritage lines

ROYAL SCOT CLASS

When formed in 1923, the London Midland & Scottish Railway faced a dilemma. It had inherited nearly ten thousand locomotives from around four hundred classes but none of them was powerful enough to cope with the heavy expresses that were being introduced on the West Coast Main Line. There was intense rivalry with the London & North Eastern Railway to gain the fastest journey times between London and Scotland, and the shortfall had to be addressed urgently. The company's Chief Mechanical Engineer, Henry Fowler, began designing a compound Pacific but after trials with a Great Western Railway Castle Class locomotive on the LMS in 1926, it was abandoned. The LMS hierarchy was so impressed by the performance of the Castle Class that they attempted to purchase fifty but this was rejected. However, they successfully obtained plans of the Lord Nelson Class from the Southern Railway, and many similarities in design could be seen when the LMS produced its own powerful 4-6-0 express locomotive.

A contract to build fifty locomotives was placed with the North British Locomotive Company, Glasgow, who worked jointly with the LMS to finalise the design. The first engine emerged in 1927 and was named *Royal Scot*, from which the class took its name. The class entered service immediately and, despite some early weaknesses, put in fine performances on express services between London and the north west, a responsibility they held until the mid-1930s. A further twenty were ordered in 1930, and these were built at Derby Works. In 1933, one member of the class (renumbered and renamed as the original *Royal Scot*) conducted a tour of major North American cities, and was displayed at an international exhibition in Chicago.

Between 1943 and 1955 the class was substantially rebuilt with tapered boilers, new frames, and cylinders, which gave them a more modern appearance and a new lease of life. All were operational in the early 1960s, and the last was withdrawn in December 1965.

6100 *Royal Scot* (unrebuilt)

SPECIFICATIONS

Class: Royal Scot
Power Type: Steam
First Built: 1927 (rebuilt 1943–55)
Withdrawn: 1962–5
Designers: Henry Fowler & NBL Co.
Builders: NBL Co. Glasgow, Derby Works

Number Built: 70
Wheel Arrangement: 4-6-0
Length: 63 ft 2¾ in
Weight: 139.5 tons
Liveries: LMS (Crimson Lake, Wartime Black, Lined Black), BR (Brunswick Green)
Names: Locomotive pioneers, British Army regiments
Preserved: 2

KING CLASS

The Great Western Railway responded quickly when its Castle Class lost the honour of being the most powerful locomotives in Britain, following the introduction of the Southern Railway's Lord Nelson Class in 1926. By this time, track and infrastructure improvements had allowed heavier designs to be considered for use on the GWR's principal routes, so Charles Collett set about designing the natural successor to his highly successful Castles. The result, dubbed the 'Super Castle', was a locomotive with a larger boiler and cylinders, yet smaller-diameter driving wheels to improve adhesion. The prototype was built with great haste in 1927 so that it could be sent to the USA to participate in the Baltimore and Ohio Railroad's centenary celebrations. The original intention was to name the class after British cathedrals, but in light of the publicity to be gained from this high-profile visit, it was decided to name the first engine after the reigning monarch, *King George V*. With a tractive effort of over 40,000 pounds, the King Class, as it became known, was capable of over 100 mph, and the GWR regained the prestigious title that the Castles had recently lost. *King George V* was a star attraction in the USA, and returned with commemorative plaques and a large bell, which have remained on the engine ever since.

Initially a total of thirty locomotives were built, and they were put in charge of the top-link expresses between London, Plymouth, and Wolverhampton. Some of their best performances were over the demanding South Devon Banks. In 1936, one locomotive (No. 6007 *King William III*) was written off following a serious accident at Shrivenham, and had to be substantially rebuilt. The outward appearance of the Kings changed little during their lives, the fitting of double chimneys from 1955 being the most obvious modification. Others included improved superheaters and mechanical lubricators. Following a major refurbishment programme in the mid-1950s, the Kings continued to reign supreme on the former GWR lines of British Railways, until replaced by the introduction of diesel hydraulic locomotives in 1962.

6000 *King George V*

SPECIFICATIONS

Class: King
Power Type: Steam
First Built: 1927
Withdrawn: 1962 (1 reinstated in 1963)
Designers: C. B. Collett BR (Blue, Green)
Builder: GWR Swindon

Number Built: 30 (1 rebuilt in 1936)
Wheel Arrangement: 4-6-0
Length: 68 ft 2 in
Weight: 135.7 tons
Liveries: GWR (various)
Names: British kings
Preserved: 3 (1 on static display at Steam Museum, Swindon)

GRESLEY CLASS A3

The Gresley Class A3 Pacifics were an evolution of the Gresley Class A1 Pacifics that were introduced in 1922. Although they shared the same chassis design, they were fitted with higher-pressure boilers and cabs with left-hand drive to improve the driver's sighting of signals. Twenty-seven A3s were built from scratch and fifty-one were converted from A1s. *Flying Scotsman* was one of the latter. It was also one of the first locomotives to be coupled to the innovative corridor tender that allowed crews to change over en route, through a connection with the leading carriage. From 1928, this allowed the first non-stop running of services between London and Scotland.

Most of the class were named after famous racehorses, but *Flying Scotsman* was one of the few exceptions, as it was named after the train that had been running since 1862. The naming took place prior to the locomotive being put on display at the British Empire Exhibition in 1924. The A3s were elegant and well proportioned locomotives that could reach speeds of 100 mph plus. Indeed it was *Flying Scotsman* (as a modified Class A1) that went on to be credited with the world's first officially recorded speed of 100 mph on 30 November 1934. This claim to fame was short-lived, as a few months later, another A3, No. 2750 *Papyrus*, reached a top speed of 108 mph between Newcastle and Kings Cross.

Gresley Class A3s marked an important chapter in British railway history as they confirmed the need for large boilers and fireboxes to provide adequate margins of steam, and hence power and efficiency, for the increasing demands of railway traffic in the early twentieth century. In later years, some of the class received improvements that altered their appearance. These modifications included the fitting of a kylchap double blastpipe and chimney, and German-style smoke deflectors (as shown).

After forty years of loyal and reliable service, only one member of the class was preserved – the most famous of them all – *Flying Scotsman*.

60103 *Flying Scotsman*

SPECIFICATIONS

Class: A3
Power Type: Steam
First Built: 1928
Withdrawn: 1959–66
Designer: Nigel Gresley
Builder: Doncaster Works

Number Built: 78 (51 rebuilt from A1)
Wheel Arrangement: 4-6-2 (Pacific)
Length: 70 ft 5 in
Weight: Approx 150 tons (full)
Liveries: LNER (Apple Green, Wartime Black), BR (Experimental Purple, BR Blue, BR Green)
Names: Most after famous racehorses
Preserved: 1 (*Flying Scotsman* at National Railway Museum)

HALL CLASS

After the formation of the 'Big Four' in 1923, the Great Western Railway was looking for a powerful mixed-traffic locomotive to cope with the increasing weight and speed of main line freight and semi-fast passenger trains. Charles Collett's plan involved rebuilding a Saint Class locomotive with smaller driving wheels, and a cab similar to the one fitted to the Castle Class. The engine began trials in 1924, and underwent three years of evaluation before the design was finalised. An order was placed for eighty locomotives, and they became known as the Hall Class. Deliveries commenced in 1928, and they proved to be so successful that another twenty were ordered, and these were followed by several more batches. Building continued until 1943, by which time 258 were in service, one having been destroyed in a bombing raid on Plymouth in 1941.

Collett's successor, Fredrick Hawksworth, ordered the building of another seventy-one locomotives to a modified design. These were built between 1943 and 1950, and became known as the Modified Halls. Although very similar in appearance, they incorporated a number of new features brought about by modern manufacturing practices and advances in steam efficiency. The Modified Halls were delivered with Hawksworth's neater but less elegant tender, but over the course of time these were interchanged throughout the class with the older Collett version. The Halls held the mantle as the GWR's standard, mixed-traffic locomotive during the steam era, and could be seen all over the network except on lines restricted by their weight.

A Modified Hall, No. 6998 *Burton Agnes Hall*, had the honour of being in charge of the last steam-hauled passenger service on BR's Western Region on 3 January 1966. One of the eighteen survivors, No. 4942 *Maindy Hall*, is being rebuilt as a Saint Class locomotive and another, No. 7927 *Willington Hall*, is being used as a donor engine for the Grange Class and County Class new build projects to fill gaps in the list of preserved GWR locomotive classes.

7930 Foremarke Hall

SPECIFICATIONS

Class: Hall/Modified Hall
Power Type: Steam
First Built: 1928 (Modified Hall 1944)
Withdrawn: 1960–5 (1 in Jan 1966)
Designers: C. B. Collett/F. W. Hawksworth
Builder: GWR Swindon

Number Built: 330 (includes 71 Modified Halls)
Wheel Arrangement: 4-6-0
Length: 63 ft ¼ in
Weight: 122.7 tons (Modified Hall – 123.1 tons)
Liveries: GWR (various including Wartime Black) BR (Green, Black)
Names: English and Welsh country halls
Preserved: 18 (2 are donor locomotives for new build projects)

5700 CLASS PANNIER TANK

9642

SPECIFICATIONS

Power Type: Steam
First Built/Withdrawn: 1929/1956–66
Designer: C. B. Collett
Builders: Swindon Works and several other builders
Number Built: 863 (*1975)
Wheel Arrangement: 0-6-0T
Length/Weight: 31 ft 2 in/48.3 tons (full)
Liveries: GWR (Green and Black), BR (mainly Black) LT (Maroon), NCB (Light Green)
Preserved: 16

The Great Western Railway was unique among the major British railway companies in adopting the Pannier Tank as the design for their standard shunter. The most prolific of these was the 5700 Class, which was based on a late-nineteenth-century design, and had water tanks attached either side of the boiler as panniers. A space above the running plate allowed ease of maintenance. They enjoyed almost twenty years of uninterrupted construction, and became the largest class in the GWR. As most were fitted with carriage heating equipment, these sprightly little engines were ideal for use on branch-line passenger services. A few of the class were fitted with condensing apparatus, which allowed them to work in the tunnels of London Transport's Metropolitan Line. Although ousted by diesel shunters, many Pannier Tanks survived until the early 1960s. London Transport purchased thirteen from British Railways for use on works trains, and the National Coal Board bought five, giving a few members of the class a new lease of life.

14XX CLASS

1466

SPECIFICATIONS

Power Type: Steam
First Built/Withdrawn: 1932/1965
Designer: C. B. Collett
Builders: GWR Swindon
Number Built: 75
Wheel Arrangement: 0-4-2T
Length/Weight: 29 ft 11 in/41.3 tons
Liveries: GWR (Green, Black), BR (Green, Black)
Preserved: 4 (1 static at Tiverton)

Although credited to Charles Collett, the design of the diminutive 14XX Class tank locomotive dates back to the nineteenth century. It was an improved version of the 517 Class introduced by George Armstrong in 1868. They were originally known as the 48XX Class but were reclassified in 1946. As a sprightly, lightweight tank engine they were perfect for GWR branch lines, and were designed to work with an auto-coach. This allowed the driver to control the engine from a cab in the coach, and avoided the need to uncouple the engine to run round its train at destinations.

The class played a starring role in the film *The Titfield Thunderbolt* (1953), where a group of villagers attempt to save their branch line from closure. In later years, when in British Railways ownership, some of the class were painted in a smart, lined-out, passenger livery. However, branch line closures and the introduction of Diesel Multiple Units took their toll, and most had been sent to scrapyards by the mid-1960s, with only a few saved for preservation.

PRINCESS ROYAL CLASS

The London Midland and Scottish Railway inherited very few powerful express locomotives when it was formed in 1923. The situation was eased by the introduction of the Royal Scot Class in 1927, but they did not match the performance of the Great Western Railway's Castle Class or the London and North Eastern Railway's Class A1. William Stanier, who joined the LMS as its Chief Mechanical Engineer in 1932, put his previous experience with the GWR into designing a Pacific to handle the heavy and demanding services on the West Coast Main Line between London and Scotland. By mid-1933, the first locomotive had been built, and the GWR influence was obvious, with many dimensions, including those of the driving wheels and cylinders, being identical to the King Class. However, Stanier had included a larger boiler and wider firebox to gain better results from inferior grades of coal. The first two locomotives were named *Princess Royal* (No. 6200) and *Princess Elizabeth* (No. 6201), and they became known as the Princess Royal Class (or 'Lizzies' in railway circles). In 1935, the class was increased to thirteen, including one (No. 6202), which had been built as an experimental turbine-driven engine known as the 'Turbomotive'. It was rebuilt as a conventional locomotive between 1950 and 1952, and named *Princess Anne,* but was destroyed in a tragic disaster involving a three-train collision at Harrow, only eight weeks after re-entering service. Later modifications to the class included the fitting of more efficient boilers and larger tenders.

In 1936, *Princess Elizabeth* broke the record for the fastest non-stop run between London and Glasgow, a distance of 401.4 miles. It achieved this in under six hours on two consecutive days, in both directions, at an average speed of 69 mph. Also in that year, the fastest speed by a member of the class was recorded – 102.5 mph by No. 6203 *Princess Margaret Rose*. This capability ensured that the Princess Royals remained in charge of top Anglo-Scottish services until they were replaced by diesels in the early 1960s.

6201 *Princess Elizabeth*

SPECIFICATIONS

Class: Princess Royal
Power Type: Steam
First Built: 1933
Withdrawn: 1962 (1 destroyed in 1952)
Designer: William Stanier
Builder: Crewe Works

Number Built: 13 (including the 'Turbomotive')
Wheel Arrangement: 4-6-2 (Pacific)
Length: 74 ft 4¼ in
Weight: 160.15 tons
Liveries: LMS (Crimson Lake, Lined Black), Wartime Black, BR (Blue, Crimson Lake, Green)
Names: Female royalty
Preserved: 2

STANIER BLACK 5

William Stanier became the Chief Mechanical Engineer of the London Midland & Scottish Railway in 1932. Previously he had served as Assistant Chief Mechanical Engineer for the Great Western Railway, and he brought with him a wealth of knowledge about locomotive practice and standardisation. This influence could be clearly seen in his design for a powerful and capable mixed-traffic locomotive. With its tapered superheated boiler, large firebox, two cylinders, and a 4-6-0 wheel arrangement, it closely resembled the GWR Hall Class. The LMS called it simply the Stanier Class 5, but later it became known more affectionately as the Black 5. Introduced in 1934, they were relatively simple locomotives with good steaming qualities, an ample tender, economic operation, and ease of maintenance. They were highly regarded by railwaymen, and such was their demand that the LMS could not build them fast enough. Construction was farmed out to independent companies, including Armstrong Whitworth of Newcastle, who built 327 of the 842 in the class.

Initially, the Black 5s were put to work on the demanding line through the Highlands between Perth and Inverness, where they transformed both passenger and freight services. They were highly versatile machines and were widely spread throughout the British railway network, particularly after nationalisation in 1948. With such a large class of locomotives, it is unsurprising that a number received modifications. These were done mainly to improve boiler and valve gear efficiency. Notably, the last two locomotives were built with outside Caprotti valve gear, which required higher running plates above the wheels and cylinders. Together with a double chimney these two engines had a distinctive appearance that represented the ultimate form of Stanier's original masterpiece.

The Black 5s were very successful and purposeful machines that outlived other more modern designs. Several saw service until the end of steam on British Railways. Indeed, the last steam-hauled passenger service was credited to a Black 5, No. 45110, on 11 August 1968.

45457

SPECIFICATIONS

Class: Stanier Black 5
Power Type: Steam
First Built: 1934
Withdrawn: 1961–8
Designer: William Stanier
Builder: Armstrong Whitworth, Crewe Works (and others)

Number Built: 842
Wheel Arrangement: 4-6-0
Length: 63 ft 7¾ in
Weight: 125.75 tons
Liveries: LMS (Black), BR (Black, Lined Black)
Names: 4 named after Scottish regiments (6 named in preservation)
Preserved: 18 (1 at National Railway Museum, Shildon)

GRESLEY CLASS P2

By the early 1930s the most powerful locomotives in the LNER inventory, the Class A3s, could not cope with the 500-ton-plus trains that had been introduced on the route between Edinburgh and Aberdeen. This was due to the line's steep gradients and tight curves, so Nigel Gresley set about designing a more powerful version of the A3, with a 2-8-2 wheel arrangement and a larger boiler.

The first locomotive, No. 2001, was built in 1934 and it was designated Class P2. Named *Cock o' the North*, the nickname of a Scottish aristocrat, it was a highly impressive machine, with a streamlined front end to deflect the exhaust from the driver's vision. A few months after entering service, the engine was sent to the French locomotive test facility at Vitry, and although its boiler efficiency proved to be good, the valve gear was found to be uneconomical. The second locomotive was therefore built with more efficient valves, and the first was modified subsequently. The next four locomotives to emerge were built with wedge-shaped front ends, similar to those introduced on the Class A4s. Only six Class P2s were built, and their magnificent appearance was marred by mechanical failures and poor efficiency. In 1943 a controversial rebuilding programme was introduced by Gresley's successor, Edward Thompson. Although many of the original parts were retained, the engines had a very different visual appearance, as they were transformed into 4-6-2 Pacifics with shorter frames and boilers. They were reclassified as Class A2/2, but they did not live up to expectations and, in 1949, were transferred to less arduous duties south of the border. Being the least economical of all the ex-LNER Pacifics, they were some of the first to be withdrawn, and all were scrapped by the early 1960s.

All being well, at least one new build Class P2 will return to the main line. A seventh member of the class, No. 2007 *Prince of Wales*, is being constructed by the P2 Steam Locomotive Company, and the Doncaster P2 Locomotive Trust plans to build a replica of No. 2001 *Cock o' the North*.

2001 *Cock o' the North*

SPECIFICATIONS

Class: P2
Power Type: Steam
First Built: 1934
Withdrawn: 1959–61 (as Class A2/2)
Designer: Nigel Gresley
Builder: Doncaster Works

Number Built: 6 (all rebuilt to Class A2/2)
Wheel Arrangement: 2-8-2 (Mikado)
Length: 74 ft 5½ in
Weight: 167.2 tons
Liveries: LNER (Apple Green, Wartime Black), BR (Green, as Class A2/2)
Names: All associated with Scotland
Preserved: 0 (1 new build and 1 replica under construction)

JUBILEE CLASS

As part of the London Midland & Scottish Railway's standardisation policy, William Stanier introduced a main line passenger locomotive intended for wide route availability, particularly on the lines that were unsuitable for the heavier Royal Scot Class. They were a tapered boiler development of the Patriot Class, and had similar lines to his mixed-traffic Black 5s, but boasted larger driving wheels, three cylinders, and a superior power output. When they first entered service in 1934, their performance was disappointing due to poor steaming, but this was overcome by modifications to the blast pipe, chimney, and firebox. The class were not named initially, but in 1935 a newly built locomotive, No. 5642, exchanged identities with the first member of the class, No. 5552, and was specially turned out in black livery with chrome embellishments. It was named *Silver Jubilee* to commemorate the Silver Jubilee of King George V, and from then on they became known as the Jubilee Class. Initially, the locomotives were delivered with Fowler 3,500-gallon tenders, but most were replaced with Stanier's standard 4,000-gallon tender.

The Jubilees were hardworking engines capable of fast running, and were used all over the LMS network. They were a common sight on the main line from St Pancras to the Midlands, the West Coast Main Line, and the cross-country routes between Bristol, Birmingham, Leeds, and York. In 1942, two Jubilees (Nos. 5735 *Comet* and 5736 *Phoenix*) were rebuilt with larger, higher-pressure boilers and double chimneys. These served as test-beds for the rebuilding of the Royal Scot and Patriot classes, and although highly successful, no further Jubilees were rebuilt. A few of the class received double chimneys and British Railways fitted four locomotives with them in 1961. The majority of the class survived until the early to mid-1960s, an exception being No. 45637 *Windward Islands*, which was damaged beyond economic repair in the tragic accident involving three passenger trains at Harrow & Wealdstone on 8 October 1952.

5690 *Leander*

SPECIFICATIONS

Class: Jubilee
Power Type: Steam
First Built: 1934
Withdrawn: 1960–7 (1 destroyed in 1952)
Designer: William Stanier
Builder: Crewe & Derby Works, NBL Co.

Number Built: 191 (includes 2 rebuilds)
Wheel Arrangement: 4-6-0
Length: 64 ft 8¾ in
Weight: 134.2 tons
Liveries: LMS (Crimson Lake, Wartime Black, Lined Black) BR (Lined Black, Lined Green)
Names: British colonies, Royal Navy admirals and warships
Preserved: 4

GRESLEY CLASS A4

Nigel Gresley's magnificent Class A3s paved the way for an even better design to meet the LNER's requirement for a locomotive to haul its prestigious Silver Jubilee trains. There was still intense rivalry between the LNER and the LMS to gain the fastest service between London and Scotland, so high speed was a vital element of the design. There was also increasing interest in diesel power following its introduction on express passenger services in Germany and Gresley was determined to show that steam was still the order of the day.

In 1935 the first Class A4, No. 2509 *Silver Link*, emerged from Doncaster Works in a striking three-tone grey livery. Essentially it was a refined A3 with a wedge-shaped streamlined casing, which had been inspired by a Bugatti rail-car that Gresley had observed in France. Unlike other British streamlined locomotives, the A4s were successful in lifting the exhaust clear of the driver's cab, and were one of the few classes of streamlined steam locomotives in the world to retain this feature throughout their existence.

During a trial run with the Silver Jubilee train, *Silver Link* achieved a maximum speed of 112.5 mph and an average speed of over 100 mph on a 43-mile stretch; both were world records at the time. Following the success of the Silver Jubilee, more streamlined services were introduced in 1937 – the Coronation which ran between London and Edinburgh, and the West Riding which ran between London, Leeds, and Bradford.

Another thirty-one A4s were built and those allocated to the Coronation services were adorned in a Garter Blue livery that later became standard for the whole class. On 3 July 1938, No. 4468 *Mallard*, which was the first of the class to be built with a Kylchap double chimney, set a world record of 126 mph while hauling six coaches and a dynamometer car (to record an accurate speed) between Grantham and Peterborough. That record has never been broken by a steam locomotive.

2509 *Silver Link*

SPECIFICATIONS

Class: A4
Power Type: Steam
First Built: 1935
Withdrawn: 1962–6 (1 destroyed in 1942)
Designer: Nigel Gresley
Builder: Doncaster Works
Number Built: 35

Wheel Arrangement: 4-6-2 (Pacific)
Length: 71 ft ½ in
Weight: Approx 168.4 tons (full)
Liveries: LNER (3-tone Grey, Garter Blue, Apple Green, Wartime Black), BR (Blue and Green)
Names: Silver 'themes', birds, LNER directors and 1 after the designer, *Sir Nigel Gresley*
Preserved: 6 (3 static: 1 at NRM, York, 1 in Canada, 1 in USA)

The onset of World War II saw the end of glamorous trains and record-breaking attempts. The A4s lost some of their streamlining to ease maintenance. They also lost their distinctive chime whistles because it was thought that these might be confused with air-raid sirens, but these were replaced after the war. One locomotive, No. 4469 *Sir Ralph Wedgwood*, was lost on 29 April 1942 due to bomb damage, although its tender survived.

In 1948, attempts were made to restart non-stop services between London and Edinburgh, but due to serious flooding and the collapse of a number of bridges on the northern sector of East Coast Main Line during August, trains had to be diverted over the Settle to Carlisle line and the Waverley route. It was during this period that A4, No. 60028 *Walter K. Wigham*, ran from Edinburgh to Kings Cross, setting a British non-stop distance record for steam of 408.65 miles. Pre-war speeds were never regained, although on 23 May 1959, No. 60007 *Sir Nigel Gresley* set a post-war British steam speed record of 112 mph. Instances of high-speed running in excess of 100 mph were common for the A4s, and no other class of steam locomotive could match them. They became affectionately known by enthusiasts and locospotters as 'Streaks'.

The class continued to give superb performances in the British Railways era, and remained on top-link duties until being replaced by the Deltics in the 1960s. The first engines to be withdrawn and scrapped were from Kings Cross shed in 1962, and the last passenger service to be hauled by an A4 (No. 60024 *Kingfisher*) was on 14 September 1966 between Aberdeen and Glasgow.

Such was their popularity that more A4s have been preserved than any other class of LNER locomotive. Three have seen regular use on the main line, two were presented to museums in North America, and *Mallard* remains a national treasure. In 2013, all six surviving A4s were brought together for the Great Gathering at the National Railway Museum, York, to celebrate the seventy-fifth anniversary of *Mallard*'s unbeaten record-breaking run.

4468 *Mallard*

60007 *Sir Nigel Gresley*

GRESLEY CLASS V2

Competition from road haulage during the 1930s spurred on the London & North Eastern Railway's ambition to introduce fast, overnight-express freight services. Introduced by Nigel Gresley in 1936, the Class V2s were highly successful mixed-traffic locomotives intended for this purpose. They incorporated a number of standard features, and much of their heritage was attributed to the designs of Classes P2 and A1/A3. However, Gresley broke new ground with a 2-6-2 wheel arrangement, which allowed the rear pony truck (known as a Cartazzi) to support a wide firebox similar to that carried by the A3. The driving wheels were identical in size to those of the P2, and the three-cylinders were capable of turning them at high speeds while providing excellent adhesion. The V2s were the only 2-6-2 tender locomotive mass produced in Britain (although there were many tank locomotive designs).

The first member of the class was named *Green Arrow*, to give publicity to a new Anglo-Scottish bulk freight and parcels service of the same name. It was soon found that the V2s performed equally well on express passenger and freight duties. During World War II they achieved some astonishing feats of haulage, and gained the reputation of being 'the engine that won the war'. In March 1940, one V2 is recorded as hauling a train of twenty-six coaches packed with troops from Peterborough to Kings Cross. They could compete with the A3 Pacifics and often deputised for them. Their only shortcomings were the restrictions imposed on route availability due to a heavy axle loading.

Although the V2s were generally reliable, a few modifications were necessary during their careers. The pony truck for the leading axle was redesigned following a series of derailments and, for seventy-one locomotives, the monobloc cylinder casting was replaced with individual cylinder castings to overcome fractured components. A few V2s were fitted with Kylchap exhausts and double chimneys, which gave them a comparable performance to the A3 Pacifics, but this enhancement arrived too late for the whole fleet to be modified.

4771 Green Arrow

SPECIFICATIONS

Power Type: Steam
First Built: 1936
Withdrawn: 1962–6
Designer: Nigel Gresley
Builders: Doncaster & Darlington Works
Number Built: 184

Wheel Arrangement: 2-6-2
Length: 66 ft 51/8 in
Weight: 144.1 tons
Liveries: LNER (Apple Green, Wartime Black), BR (Black, Lined Black, Lined Green)
Names: *Green Arrow*, Army regiments (5), schools (2)
Preserved: 1 (*Green Arrow* at National Railway Museum)

PRINCESS CORONATION CLASS

The introduction of Nigel Gresley's Class A4s and streamlined trains on the East Coast Main Line intensified the rivalry between the LNER and the LMS in the mid-1930s. When the LMS began to slip behind due to a lack of suitably powerful express locomotives, William Stanier took steps to improve upon his Princess Royal Class. The new locomotives were specifically intended to haul the prestigious Coronation Scot express services between London and Glasgow, in direct competition with the LNER's Coronation expresses that ran between London and Edinburgh. Both of these trains were named to commemorate the coronation of King George VI in 1937. The problem for Stanier was that the West Coast Main Line had challenging gradients, particularly over the summits at Shap and Beattock, so a large boiler and firebox were essential.

The first locomotive, suitably adorned in a streamline casing and a striking blue livery with silver lining to match the Coronation Scot's special coaches, emerged from Crewe Works in 1937 looking magnificent. It was named *Coronation* and, in light of their heritage, the production of further locomotives led to them becoming known as the Princess Coronation Class (although footplate crews nicknamed them the 'Big Lizzies'). The second batch of locomotives were painted in Crimson Lake, with lining in gold, vermilion, and black to match the livery of the standard LMS coaches. Not all of the class were built as streamliners – fourteen of the thirty-eight were built as conventional locomotives. Although the design was credited to Stanier, much of it, and particularly the streamlining, was attributable to Derby's Chief Draughtsman, Tom Coleman. An unusual feature of the Coronation Class was that their tenders were fitted with a steam-operated coal pusher to bring coal forward from the back of the tender. This equipment greatly helped the fireman to meet the high demands of the fire.

During trials with a special train in June 1937, *Coronation* achieved a speed of 114 mph, which broke the British speed

6220 *Coronation* (streamlined)

SPECIFICATIONS

Class: Princess Coronation
Power Type: Steam
First Built: 1937
Withdrawn: 1962–4
Designer: William Stanier
Builder: Crewe Works
Number Built: 38

Wheel Arrangement: 4-6-2 (Pacific)
Length: 73 ft 10¼ in
Weight: 160.15 tons full (164.45 streamlined)
Liveries: LMS (Crimson Lake, Lined Black), Black BR (Lined Black, Blue, Crimson Lake, Green)
Names: Royalty, duchesses, British cities, and *Sir William A. Stanier FRS*, named after the designer
Preserved: 3 (1 static at Birmingham Museum)

record of 112.5 mph set by the LNER's *Silver Link* in September 1935. However, glory was short-lived for the LMS because the record was smashed by the LNER's *Mallard* in July 1938. A further trial in February 1939 with No. 6234 *Duchess of Abercorn*, which was unstreamlined and had been fitted with a double chimney, demonstrated the full capability of the class. Hauling a train of twenty coaches and over 600 tons between Crewe and Glasgow, it sustained in excess of 3,300 horsepower for five minutes and became the most powerful steam locomotive ever to run on British rails. However, to achieve this feat, it required two firemen to shovel coal into the fire at a fast enough rate.

In January 1939, No. 6229 *Duchess of Hamilton* swapped identities with No. 6220 *Coronation* for a tour of the USA, which included being put on public display at the World Trade Fair in New York. During this visit it carried a large headlight and bell at the front of the locomotive. Due to the outbreak of World War II, the locomotive became stranded in the country and did not return to England until 1942, whereupon it resumed its true identity.

The Princess Coronations were an excellent design from the outset, and few modifications were necessary, although double chimneys were fitted from 1939, and smoke deflectors became standard from 1945. The locomotives fitted with streamlining had it removed from 1946 onwards, as it offered little towards improving overall performance, and caused difficulties with access for maintenance. The last two members of the class were built with modifications made by Stanier's successor, H. G. Ivatt. These included a new type of superheater, Timken roller bearings, a self-cleaning smoke box, and a substantially redesigned lower rear end and trailing truck.

The Princess Coronations, widely regarded as Stanier's ultimate masterpiece, were the most powerful passenger steam locomotives ever to be built for the LMS network. Ironically, when withdrawn in the early 1960s, they were more powerful than the diesels that replaced them.

6229 *Duchess of Hamilton* (streamlined)

46229 *Duchess of Hamilton* (unstreamlined)

MERCHANT NAVY CLASS

During the 1930s, the Southern Railway had fallen behind the other major railway companies in modernising its fleet of ageing locomotives. However, in 1937, Oliver Bulleid was appointed as its Chief Mechanical Engineer, and he had spent many years as the personal assistant to Nigel Gresley. He also had extensive knowledge of locomotive developments on the Continent, so it was not surprising that his first major design was technologically advanced. It had a high-pressure boiler, and a welded steel firebox with thermic syphons to increase thermal efficiency. Bulleid enveloped the locomotive in an air-smooth casing, which blended with his own design of coaching stock, and gave it Box-pok wheels which were lighter, yet stronger, than those with spokes. He also included a number of features to assist the locomotive crew; chain-driven valve gear immersed in a sealed oil bath to reduce the burden of frequent oiling, a steam-operated fire door, an enclosed cab with excellent ergonomics, and electric lighting.

Introduced in 1941 under strict wartime conditions, the class was intended for fast passenger services in southern England, and were named after shipping companies that used the Southern Railway's docks. The colloquial name 'Spam Can' became popular with railwaymen and loco spotters due to their resemblance with the distinctive tin cans in which Spam pre-cooked meat was sold, but Merchant Navy Class was their official designation. Several versions of tender were built with water capacities varying between 5,000 and 6,000 gallons, and these were swapped frequently between engines.

Unfortunately, Bulleid's novel features caused problems and maintenance difficulties so, starting in 1956, British Railways rebuilt the entire class to a more conventional design. Although retaining the frames, wheels and boiler most of the radical features were dispensed with. The locomotives were highly attractive in their new guise and were widely regarded, in terms of performance and smooth running, as one of Britain's finest Pacifics.

35007 *Aberdeen Commonwealth* (rebuilt)

SPECIFICATIONS

Class: Merchant Navy
Power Type: Steam
First Built: 1941 (rebuilt 1956–9)
Withdrawn: 1964–7
Designer: Oliver Bulleid
Builder: Eastleigh Works

Number Built: 30
Wheel Arrangement: 4-6-2 (Pacific)
Length: 69 ft 7¾ in
Weight: Approx. 144.75 tons (rebuilt 151.5 tons)
Liveries: SR (Malachite Green, Wartime Black), BR (Malachite Green, Blue, Green)
Names: Merchant shipping companies
Preserved: 11 (1 sectioned static exhibit at National Railway Museum, York)

THOMPSON CLASS B1

Sir Nigel Gresley died after a short illness in April 1941, and was succeeded as the LNER's Chief Mechanical Engineer by Edward Thompson. Thompson had a totally different outlook on locomotive design, and was a great believer in simplicity and standardisation. Where possible he used existing LNER components including boilers, wheels, and tenders, to make savings in the austere wartime conditions. At the top of his priorities he saw the need for a powerful, mixed-traffic locomotive to replace numerous obsolescent classes from the Pre-Grouping era. Thompson came up with an unsophisticated, general purpose design that was the first two-cylinder, main-line LNER locomotive to be built since 1923 (Gresley had always favoured three-cylinders). It was a purposeful, well-proportioned locomotive that became designated Class B1, and it was the LNER's equivalent of the GWR Hall and LMS Black 5.

Production of the first ten locomotives began in 1942, but deliveries were slow due to the war. Following the end of hostilities, construction was spread across various locations, and a further four hundred were built up until 1952. The first locomotive was named *Springbok*, in connection with the visit of the South African prime minister, and, in light of their sprightly performance, it seemed appropriate to name the subsequent forty locomotives after species of antelope. Unofficially, the class were nicknamed 'Bongos' (after the name of No. 1005). The B1s could be found all over the LNER network, including the former Great Eastern, Great Northern, and Great Central lines, where they put in superb performances on top-link expresses. They were also highly successful in Scotland, due to their ability to pull away with heavy trains on steep gradients.

Undoubtedly the best of Thompson's designs, the B1s shared mixed opinions with footplate crews; they were good steamers with fast acceleration but were criticised for rough riding. Withdrawal came long before the end of their projected working lives, with some engines seeing little more than ten years' service. The last three were withdrawn in 1967.

61003 *Gazelle*

SPECIFICATIONS

Class: B1
Power Type: Steam
First Built: 1942
Withdrawn: 1961–7 (1 destroyed in 1950)
Designer: Edward Thompson
Builders: Darlington, Gorton, NBL Co., VF

Number Built: 410
Wheel Arrangement: 4-6-0
Length: 61 ft 73/8 in
Weight: 123.15 tons
Liveries: LNER (Apple Green, Wartime Black), BR (Apple Green, Lined Black)
Names: Antelope species (40), LNER directors (18), *Mayflower*
Preserved: 2 (1 in service and 1 in preservation)

WD AUSTERITY CLASS 8F

During World War II, a large number of freight locomotives were built for the War Department (WD). Initially, the Stanier Class 8F was the prime choice for this purpose, but a simpler and more economic design was sought. The intention was to have a basic design that could be built by several different builders using standard parts. Robert Arthur Riddles, a locomotive engineer who had worked under Sir William Stanier, was the Director of Transportation Equipment at the Ministry of Supply, and he introduced a radical new concept of locomotive design based on simplicity. All refinements were eliminated to ensure reliability under military operating conditions on a war-torn and poorly maintained infrastructure. The result was a locomotive with a parallel boiler, and a box tender that looked austere compared to the elegant designs that had emerged before. Hence they became known as the 'Austerities'.

Production of the Austerities was rapid thanks to their simplicity and thousands of hours were saved in construction.

At one point seven locomotives per week were being delivered. Two similar types were built between 1943 and 1945. They were identifiable by their boiler lengths and wheel arrangements: a 2-8-0 version (935 built) and a 2-10-0 version (150 built). The latter had a lighter axle loading, to make it more suitable for secondary lines. Many of the locomotives saw service in mainland Europe and in the Middle East. At the end of hostilities most were repatriated but some were sold to foreign customers. Upon the nationalisation of the railways in 1948, British Railways took ownership of 733 of the 2-8-0s, and twenty-five of the 2-10-0s, and two of each version were purchased by the Longmoor Military Railway (LMR) in Hampshire.

The Austerities were rugged and reliable locomotives that lasted much longer than envisaged, with the last BR 2-8-0 and 2-10-0 examples being withdrawn in 1962 and 1967 respectively. The Greek 2-10-0s remained in service until the late 1970s, and two of these were rescued for preservation in Great Britain.

90766

SPECIFICATIONS (2-10-0 VERSION)

Class: WD Austerity 8F
Power Type: Steam
First Built: 1943
Withdrawn: 1961–2
Designer: R. A. Riddles
Builder: NBL Co.

Number Built: 150 (25 in BR service)
Wheel Arrangement: 2-10-0
Length: 58 ft 10¼ in
Weight: 133.8 tons (full)
Liveries: WD (Khaki, Green), LMR (Blue), BR (Black)
Names: BR: North British (2), LMR: *Gordon*, *Kitchener*; in preservation: *Dame Vera Lynn*
Preserved: 4 (1 at Dutch Railway Museum, Utrecht)

WEST COUNTRY AND BATTLE OF BRITAIN CLASSES

Although highly successful in meeting the Southern Railway's need for a powerful express locomotive, Bulleid's Merchant Navy Class were too heavy for most of the Southern's key routes, so he developed a class that was scaled down and lighter. The first of this new design appeared in 1945, and it was decided to name the class after West Country towns and cities. A later batch of engines was named after famous personalities, aircraft, fighter squadrons, and airfields that had been involved in the Battle of Britain. Although split into two different classes by their names – West Country and Battle of Britain – the locomotives were identical, and collectively they were referred to as Bulleid Light Pacifics. They were delivered with Bulleid's unusual numbering system that he adopted from continental practice. Performance, in terms of haulage capacity and sustained speed, was excellent, and these fine engines worked both passenger and freight services between London, the south coast, and the south west, including the challenging Somerset & Dorset line.

After the nationalisation of the railways in 1948, a series of exchange trials were conducted which allowed certain classes from the 'Big Four' to venture into new territory. During this period, a few West Country and Battle of Britain Class locomotives found themselves a long way from home, the most notable being No. 34004 *Yeovil*, which ran on the Scottish Highland Line between Perth and Inverness.

Two significant modifications were made to the engines shortly after their introduction. The smoke deflectors were lengthened, and the cab was cut back and given larger front windows to give the crew better forward vision. Most of the novel features that Bulleid had introduced in the Merchant Navy Class were incorporated into his lighter design, which inevitably led to similar maintenance issues. To address the situation a rebuilding programme began in 1957, but for economic reasons only sixty engines were rebuilt. Modernisation brought the careers of the Bulleid Light Pacifics to an early demise, and they were all withdrawn between 1963 and 1967.

21C123 *Blackmoor Vale* (unrebuilt)

SPECIFICATIONS

Class: West Country and Battle of Britain
Power Type: Steam
First Built: 1945 (60 rebuilt 1957–9)
Withdrawn: 1963–7
Designer: Oliver Bulleid
Builder: Eastleigh and Brighton Works

Number Built: 110
Wheel Arrangement: 4-6-2 (Pacific)
Length: 67 ft 4¾ in
Weight: Approx. 128.6 tons (rebuilt – approx. 139.25 tons)
Liveries: SR (Malachite Green), BR (Malachite Green, Green)
Names: West Country towns and cities, *Sir Eustace Missenden*, RAF subjects associated with the Battle of Britain
Preserved: 20

PEPPERCORN CLASS A2

The post-war years were a turbulent time for the 'Big Four' railway companies, as they were recovering from a long period of hardship and austerity. This was particularly so for the London & North Eastern Railway, which underwent a major change in direction with the locomotive designs by Edward Thompson. He set in train a number of passenger and mixed-traffic designs that were simple and easy to maintain. These included the rebuilding of Gresley's P2 Class, which had become known as the Class A2/2, and the last four Gresley Class V2s, which were built as Pacifics and designated Class A2/1. In 1944 Thompson authorised the building of thirty Pacifics, based on the Class A2/2, and these were classified as A2/3. However, Thompson was succeeded by Arthur Peppercorn in 1946, and he made improvements to this cumbersome design. The last fifteen were built to his specification, and became known as the Peppercorn Class A2.

The first A2, No. 525 *A. H. Peppercorn*, was the last LNER Pacific to be built before the nationalisation of the railways in 1948, and appropriately, it was named after its designer. These locomotives incorporated a number of modern features, including a speedometer, electric lighting, a self-cleaning smoke box and ashpan, but somewhat surprisingly, only a single chimney. That said, the last one off the production line was fitted with a Kylchap double blast pipe, and five other engines received these retrospectively.

In terms of maintenance and efficiency, the A2s were highly cost effective, and frequently ran over 100,000 miles between major servicing. They were ideal for operating in the northern sector of the former LNER and were, best known for their work in Scotland, where they had replaced Gresley's troublesome P2s. However, they did not share the same prestige as the Gresley Pacifics because they were designed for heavy loads, rather than light, fast trains. The last three examples in service, all allocated to Dundee shed, were withdrawn in 1966 and one, No. 60532 *Blue Peter*, was secured for preservation after a successful appeal by the TV programme of the same name.

60538 *Velocity*

SPECIFICATIONS

Class: A2
Power Type: Steam
First Built: 1947
Withdrawn: 1962–6
Designer: Arthur Peppercorn
Builders: Doncaster Works

Number Built: 15
Wheel Arrangement: 4-6-2 (Pacific)
Length: 71 ft ¾ in
Weight: 161.35 tons
Liveries: LNER (Apple Green), BR (Apple Green), BR (Apple Green, Green)
Names: *A. H. Peppercorn* (1), famous racehorses (14)
Preserved: 1

PEPPERCORN CLASS A1

Unlike his predecessor, Arthur Peppercorn favoured Nigel Gresley's philosophies when it came to locomotive designs. Having refined Thompson's Class A2 design, he used this as the basis for a Pacific using the same boiler and cab, but with larger driving wheels and a Kylchap double blast pipe. Class A4-style streamlining was intended but the British Railways Executive overruled this in order to save costs. These locomotives became known as Class A1, and although a pure LNER design, they were all built after nationalisation. The first of forty-nine engines was delivered in August 1948 and all were named, albeit with a mixture of themes. They were the last in a long line of famous express passenger steam locomotives built for service on the East Coast Main Line.

Unfortunately, Peppercorn's untimely death in March 1951 meant that he saw little of the energetic work that these excellent machines performed. Although more powerful than the A4 Pacifics, and less prone to wheel slips, they did not have corridor tenders, and this prevented them from taking charge of the London to Edinburgh non-stop services. The class required few modifications during their working lives. Five locomotives were equipped with Timken roller bearings but, although very successful in increasing the time between major repairs, they were deemed too expensive to warrant fitting to the whole fleet. Some locomotives were fitted with silencers in their smoke boxes, to counter the sound of the ejectors while standing in stations.

Frugal and free steaming, the Peppercorn A1s were the most reliable and economical of all British Pacific designs. Capable of hauling fifteen coach trains at a sustained speed of 70 mph, they did sterling work in their short lives. The first was withdrawn in 1962 and the last, No. 60145 *Saint Mungo*, which had a working life of only seventeen years, was withdrawn in 1966. The entire class was scrapped, but in 2008 a brand new A1 was built to the original design, while incorporating modern main line requirements. It was given the number of the fiftieth member of the class – 60163, and named *Tornado*.

60163 *Tornado*

SPECIFICATIONS

Class: A1
Power Type: Steam
First Built: 1948 (1 new build 2008)
Withdrawn: 1962–6
Designer: Arthur Peppercorn
Builders: Doncaster & Darlington Works

Number Built: 50
Wheel Arrangement: 4-6-2 (Pacific)
Length: 72 ft 11¾ in
Weight: 170.8 tons
Liveries: BR (Apple Green, Lined Blue, Lined Green)
Names: Racehorses, prominent people, birds, railway companies, Scottish-related names, *Tornado*
Preserved: 0 (1 new build – 60163 *Tornado*)

BRITANNIA CLASS

Following the inter-regional Locomotive Exchange Trials in 1948, British Railways revealed plans for twelve standard classes of locomotive. Robert Riddles was the man in charge of locomotive procurement for the newly nationalised railways, and he began with a design for a mixed-traffic Pacific. With economy, efficiency, and ease of maintenance still fresh in his mind from the war years, he introduced the first two-cylinder main-line Pacific in Great Britain. The lack of a third cylinder and motion between the frames meant that the locomotive was lighter and easier to maintain. The design was strongly influenced by the strengths of earlier designs, most notably the Merchant Navy Class and Princess Coronation Class, and included many features considered to be best practice from the 'Big Four'. The tender was a more sophisticated version of those fitted to the WD Austerity 2-8-0 and 2-10-0 Classes (the last ten engines to be built were coupled to BR tenders that were similar to an LMS design, with increased coal capacity and a mechanical coal-pusher). The pioneer of the class emerged from Crewe Works on 2 January 1951, and was named *Britannia*. It was the first of many to receive symbolic British names that included *William Shakespeare*, *Robert Burns*, and *Charles Dickens*.

Early on, the class encountered some serious mechanical problems, but these were quickly rectified. Although not universally popular, the Britannias were excellent engines. Their introduction transformed services on the East Anglian expresses which, at one point, were the fastest services in the country. By the end of the 1950s they were seeing widespread use on all of the BR regions, and being more economical than the Merchant Navy Class, two were regularly employed on the Southern Region's prestigious Golden Arrow service. However, BR's Modernisation Plan put a stop to construction after 1954, which meant that the Britannias had very short working lives, and the bulk of the class was withdrawn in 1966–7. The last operational member of the class, No. 70013 *Oliver Cromwell*, was one of the last steam locomotives to haul a passenger train on British Railways, on 11 August 1968.

70000 *Britannia*

SPECIFICATIONS

Class: Britannia (Standard Class 7)
Power Type: Steam
First Built: 1951
Withdrawn: 1965–8
Designer: Robert Riddles
Builders: Crewe Works

Number Built: 55
Wheel Arrangement: 4-6-2 (Pacific)
Length: 68 ft 9 in
Weight: 143.15 tons
Liveries: BR (Lined Green, Unlined Green)
Names: Great Britons, former Star Class locomotives, Scottish firths (70047 was unnamed)
Preserved: 2

STANDARD CLASS 5

The twelve Standard Classes that were introduced by Robert Riddles bore a strong family resemblance to each other with their tapered boilers, two cylinders, high running plates, streamlined cabs, and standard fittings. Labour-saving devices were also a common feature, some of which had been gained from experience with the American S160 locomotives that had operated in Britain during World War II. Of note, self-cleaning smoke boxes became standard, which meant that smoke-box doors only had to be opened for boiler examinations and wash outs. The most powerful Standard engines, the Pacifics, were all given wide fireboxes to provide good steaming, but the mixed-traffic and freight locomotives had narrow fireboxes to avoid the need for a trailing truck. Visually, the LMS influence was obvious in the Standard Class 5, which was heavily based on the Stanier Black 5. However, the improvements that Riddles introduced made them much more capable machines.

There were some notable differences among the class. Firstly, six different types of tender were fitted depending on operating requirements (for example, locomotives allocated to the Southern Region were attached to tenders with a greater water capacity, to overcome the lack of water troughs). Secondly, thirty locomotives were built with Caprotti valve gear and poppet valves. Developed from an Italian design, the operation of this system depended on cam shafts rather than piston valves and, although more complex and difficult to maintain, gave a distinct power advantage over the conventional engines. Only twenty locomotives were named in service, all belonged to the Southern Region, and they took their names from withdrawn King Arthur Class engines.

The Standard Class 5s were allocated to all regions of the British Railways network, and were universally popular with crews due to their excellent performance and reliability. They could be found on diverse duties, from short pick-up freights to main-line expresses, and often substituted for Pacifics. The class worked many of BR's last steam-hauled passenger services.

73005

SPECIFICATIONS

Class: Standard Class 5
Power Type: Steam
First Built: 1951
Withdrawn: 1964–8
Designer: Robert Riddles
Builders: Derby and Doncaster Works

Number Built: 172
Wheel Arrangement: 4-6-0
Length: 62 ft 7 in
Weight: 125.15 tons (with BR1 tender)
Liveries: BR (Lined and Unlined Black, Lined Green)
Names: Former King Arthur Class locomotives (20), *City of Peterborough* (in preservation)
Preserved: 5

STANDARD CLASS 4 TANK

The Standard Class 4 Tank was the most numerous of the standard tank locomotives built by British Railways. It was based on the well-proven and highly versatile Stanier and Fairburn designs that had been constructed in large numbers for the LMS between 1935 and 1951. With their free steaming, excellent acceleration, and smooth riding characteristics, they were ideally suited for commuter and suburban traffic. Initially allocated to all regions of British Railways except the Western, with the Southern and Scottish gaining large numbers to replace older types, they were much admired by both footplate crews and maintenance staff.

The majority of the class were built at the former LBSCR Works at Brighton, and two smaller batches were built at Derby and Doncaster Works. The full order was not completed; fifteen were cancelled due to the modernisation programme that curtailed the manufacturing of steam locomotives. When designed, it was expected that these large tank engines would be required to spend considerable time operating bunker first, to save time turning them between tightly scheduled commuter services. To that end, the coal bunker was designed with an inset to give the crew good forward visibility from the cab when running in reverse. Apart from minor differences to the coupling rods and their fittings, no other modifications were made to the class.

The Standard Class 4 Tanks were one of the most successful of the BR Standard designs, and did sterling work on the suburban services between London, Tilbury, and Southend. They were also intensively used on the commuter lines around Glasgow, and on local services in Kent and East Sussex. However, they were struck down in their youth and all were retired by mid-1967. With much useful life remaining, many of these versatile tank locomotives were fortunate to escape the cutter's torch, and have found new homes on heritage railways. At the time of writing, all but three of the fifteen preserved locomotives have been operational, with four having seen service on the main line.

80154

SPECIFICATIONS

Class: Standard Class 4 Tank
Power Type: Steam
First Built: 1951
Withdrawn: 1962–?
Designer: Robert Riddles
Builders: Brighton, Derby, Doncaster Works

Number Built: 155
Wheel Arrangement: 2-6-4T
Length: 44 ft 9 ⁷/₈ in
Weight: 86.65 tons (full)
Liveries: BR (Lined and Unlined Black, Lined Green [in preservation only])
Names: None
Preserved: 15

CLASS 08

From the mid-1930s the LMS had been attracted by the economy and instant availability of diesel traction. They acquired a number of prototype diesel locomotives, and among the most successful was a shunter designed by the English Electric Co., which had six coupled wheels driven by a 350-hp engine and electric transmission. Although there were small production runs of these machines both before and during World War II, it was not until after the war that serious production began. After nationalisation in 1948, British Railways carried out an evaluation of the type and decided that the design, with some minor modifications, was ideal to meet its shunter requirements. This was the genesis of what would later be known as the Class 08 diesel shunter, and with 996 being built between 1952 and 1962, it was the most numerous of all British locomotive classes.

Over the years, many minor modifications were made to the class to enhance their utility and to prolong their lives. Some were fitted with radios to enable communications between the driver and controllers in large marshalling yards. Other modifications included the fitting of waterproof cab doors to enable their use through carriage-washing plants, different headlights for specific routes, and roof-mounted flashing warning beacons. A modification reflecting advances in technology in the twenty-first century was the installation of remote-control equipment, allowing locomotives to be driven by a member of staff remote from the locomotive. The most extraordinary modification of all involved the permanent coupling of two Class 08s, with the cab of the leading locomotive being removed to form a permanently coupled 'master and slave' unit. Known as Class 13, three of these combinations were used for hump-shunting duties at Tinsley marshalling yards between 1965 and 1985.

As its standard, general-purpose diesel shunter, BR deployed the Class 08 to every region of its network. The class became a familiar sight at many freight and marshalling yards, major stations, and traction maintenance depots.

However, over the course of time the nature of rail traffic changed with the introduction of fixed rakes of container wagons and passenger-carrying multiple units, which reduced the demand for shunting locomotives. Consequently, large numbers of the class were withdrawn from use and stored, scrapped, exported, or sold to industrial and heritage railways. The remaining members of the class became employed as convenient utility engines on more mundane duties than those for which they were intended. That said, it is expected that examples of this venerable war-horse will remain operational for many years to come, as no replacement is in sight.

In addition to the large number of Class 08s built, there were also twenty-six Class 09 and 146 Class 10 locomotives, which were outwardly very similar but mechanically different. The Class 09 locomotives had different gearing to provide a higher top speed at the expense of tractive effort, and the Class 10 locomotives were powered by Blackstone diesel engines and GEC traction motors. A number of locomotives based on the Class 08 design were also built for export.

D3932

SPECIFICATIONS

Class: 08
Power Type: Diesel-electric
First Built: 1952
Withdrawn: First in 1967 but several still in use as of 2016
Designer: English Electric Co.
Builders (BR): Crewe, Doncaster, Darlington, Derby, Horwich
Number Built: 996
Wheel Arrangement: 0-6-0
Length: 29 ft 3 in
Weight: 49.6 tons
Liveries: BR and its privatised constituents, various others
Preserved: 60 +

STANDARD CLASS 8

Ten of British Railways' Standard Classes were designed for general-purpose and mixed-traffic work. The other two were more specialist designs, one for heavy freight, the Standard Class 9, and the other for express passenger duties, the Standard Class 8. However, the latter was not an urgent priority, as there were already many excellent types in service. In fact the class would not have been built had it not been for the tragic accident at Harrow in October 1952, in which the Princess Royal Class locomotive No. 46202 *Princess Anne* was destroyed. This provided the opportunity to build a prototype. Unlike the other Standard Class designs it had three cylinders, and incorporated Caprotti valve gear. The boiler was similar to that used on the Britannia Class, but had an enlarged firebox and double chimney.

A few months after its delivery in May 1954, BR announced that it would phase out steam in favour of diesel and electric traction, so the locomotive that had been named *Duke of Gloucester* was the first and only Standard Class 8 to be built.

It showed a promising development in British steam locomotive development but in service the *Duke*, as it became known, was a lacklustre performer due to its poor steaming characteristics and heavy coal consumption. A new tender with greater coal capacity was built for it in 1957, but this did nothing to overcome its fundamental problems, and it was generally unpopular with crews.

After a short, disappointing career, the *Duke* was withdrawn in 1962, and stored at Crewe pending its fate. Eventually it was decided not to preserve the whole engine but to remove one of the cylinders and valve gear for static exhibition at the Science Museum in London. The remains of the locomotive were sent to Barry for scrapping, but it was rescued for preservation in 1974. After a remarkable thirteen year restoration project involving the manufacture of several new parts, including cylinders and valve gear, this unique locomotive with its initial flaws ironed out, has since been able to demonstrate its true potential on the main line.

71000 *Duke of Gloucester*

SPECIFICATIONS

Class: Standard Class 8
Power Type: Steam
First Built: 1954
Withdrawn: 1962
Designer: Robert Riddles
Builders: Crewe Works

Number Built: 1
Wheel Arrangement: 4-6-2 (Pacific)
Length: 70 ft
Weight: 156.75 tons (with BR1E tender), 154.95 tons (with BR1J tender)
Liveries: BR (Lined Green)
Name: *Duke of Gloucester*
Preserved: 1

STANDARD CLASS 9F

The last in Robert Riddles' series of Standard Class locomotives was a heavy-freight design capable of hauling trains of up to 900 tons. Known as the Standard Class 9F, it was one of the most powerful, and arguably the most successful, of all the steam locomotive types to be built in Great Britain. Key features of the design were a 2-10-0 wheel arrangement to give increased traction and a low axle loading, flangeless centre driving wheels to allow the locomotive to traverse tight-radius curves, and a highly efficient boiler.

Despite the imminent withdrawal en masse of steam locomotives on British Railways, a number of technical experiments were carried out on the 9Fs in the pursuit of further improving their power and efficiency. Three engines were built with mechanical stokers, and one was fitted with a Giesel ejector (an Austrian-designed multiple blast pipe that replaced the standard version and chimney). Ten locomotives were fitted with the distinctive but ungainly Franco-Crosti boiler (another Continental feature), which had a second drum under the main boiler to preheat the water. The hot gases passed through both and were ejected through an additional chimney mounted on the right-hand side of the boiler. None of the experiments were deemed worthy of further investment; however, double chimneys were fitted to the locomotives built in the later years and some were retrofitted to engines built earlier. Various types of the larger BR tenders were attached, depending upon requirements.

The Standard 9Fs were not only highly capable heavy-freight machines, they also put in spirited performances in charge of express services, with some being clocked at 90 mph. In this regard they were often used on relief trains and as standby locomotives. The last of the class was built at Swindon in March 1960. Carrying the number 92220 and named *Evening Star*, it was specially turned out in BR Lined Green livery with a copper-capped chimney. It was also the last steam locomotive to be built for British Railways, and had a working life of only five years before being secured as part of the National Collection.

92164

SPECIFICATIONS

Class: Standard Class 9
Power Type: Steam
First Built: 1954
Withdrawn: 1964–8
Designer: Robert Riddles
Builders: Swindon (53), Crewe (198)

Number Built: 251
Wheel Arrangement: 2-10-0
Length: 66 ft 2 in
Weight: 139.2 tons
Liveries: BR (Unlined Black, Lined Green (1))
Names: *Evening Star*, *Black Prince**, *Morning Star**, *Cock o' the North**, *Central Star* (* in preservation)
Preserved: 9

DELTIC

The English Electric Company, who had gained experience in building diesel locomotives for the export market since the 1930s, built a prototype locomotive which it loaned to British Railways in 1955 for evaluation. It was powered by two Napier Deltic engines, similar to those that had been used in naval gun boats. These were two-stroke, eighteen-cylinder engines with an output of 1,650 hp each. The power unit was a complex and compact yet light design, with three banks of cylinders in a V formation (hence the name *Deltic*, which originates from *Delta*, the Greek for 'triangle'). The locomotive was painted in a striking, powder-blue livery with aluminium trim and pale yellow embellishments. It had no number (although it was officially known as 'DP1'), and simply carried the name *Deltic*.

Initial trials took place on the London Midland Region main line between Liverpool and London, where *Deltic* gave some excellent performances. Subsequently it ran between Carlisle and Skipton, where it continued to impress but it was deemed too expensive to meet the London Midland Region's future requirements. However, the management of the Eastern Region could see the potential of the machine as a replacement for their top-link Pacifics on the East Coast Main Line, so an order was placed in 1958 for twenty-three (later reduced to twenty-two) production locomotives. A few design changes were necessary, including a reduction in the loading gauge and the fitting of improved generators and traction motors.

Deltic was transferred to Hornsey depot in 1959 so that experience with the locomotive could be gained on services from Kings Cross. Unfortunately, it suffered a serious engine failure in March 1961 and was withdrawn from service, but by then delivery of the production machines had begun. The locomotive was never taken into British Railways ownership, and after withdrawal it was donated by the English Electric Company to the Science Museum in London. In 1993 it was moved to the National Railway Museum at York, and has been on display more recently at Shildon and the Ribble Steam Railway.

Deltic

SPECIFICATIONS

Class: N/A (prototype for Class 55)
Power Type: Diesel-electric
Built: 1955
Withdrawn: 1961
Builder: English Electric Co.
Number Built: 1

Wheel Arrangement: Co-Co
Length: 66 ft
Weight: 106 tons
Max Speed: 105 mph
Livery: Unique – as shown
Name: *Deltic*
Preserved: National Railway Museum, Shildon

CLASS 20

The Modernisation Plan for British Railways was published in December 1954. Among its recommendations was the large-scale replacement of steam locomotives with diesel and electric traction. However, implementation of the plan was poorly managed, and large numbers of diesels were rushed into service without thorough testing. This resulted in shortfalls in performance and poor reliability, which led to a number of classes being withdrawn soon after their steam counterparts.

One of the most successful of the pioneer diesel classes was a design intended for light-freight duties. Known initially as the English Electric Type 1, it became the Class 20 under British Rail's Total Operating Processing System (TOPS). The initial order was for twenty locomotives but, due to the failings of other pioneer Type 1 diesels, subsequent orders took the total to 228. The design was unusual in having a single cab at one end, and this gave rise to the frequent sight of locomotives being coupled nose to nose when used in tandem operation.

Power was provided by the relatively simple but reliable 1,000-hp English Electric 8SVT unit and four traction motors. Among enthusiasts the Class 20s gained the nickname 'Choppers', due to the beat of their engines resembling the sound of helicopters. The main visual difference between the earlier and later members of the class was the train indicator systems. Initially, white discs were used, as in the steam era, but these were superseded by electric route-indicator boxes. A few Class 20s that operated over the single lines in Scotland had a tablet-catcher recess on the side of the cab. The Class 20s were predominately allocated to the London Midland, Eastern, and Scottish Regions. Although used mainly on freight trains, they hauled passenger services occasionally.

A considerable number of the class were refurbished in the early 1980s, which extended their lives into the twenty-first century. A few were involved with the construction of the Channel Tunnel, and some ventured on to the Continent. Other unusual duties have included weed killing, and nuclear flask trains.

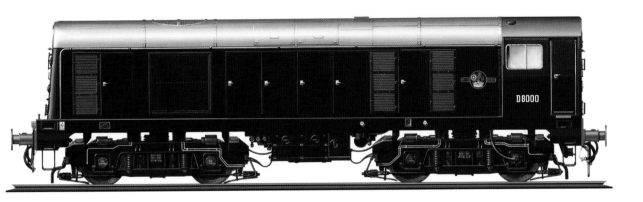

D8000

SPECIFICATIONS

Class: 20
Power Type: Diesel-electric
First Built: 1957
Withdrawn: 1981 – a few still in service (as at 2016)
Builder: English Electric Co. & RSH Ltd
Number Built: 228

Wheel Arrangement: Bo-Bo
Length: 46 ft 9¼ in
Weight: 73 tons
Max Speed: 75 mph
Liveries: BR (Green, Corporate Blue), Railfreight, DRS, HRNC, various others
Preserved: 25 (as at 2016)

CLASS 40

Under the pilot scheme of the Modernisation Plan for British Railways, ten express diesel locomotives were ordered. Many aspects of the design were based on prototype locomotives that had seen service on the London Midland and Southern Regions between 1947 and 1954. These imposing machines were powered by a 2,000-hp English Electric 16SVT engine and six traction motors with a 1Co-Co1 wheel arrangement. Train heating was provided by a steam boiler.

Originally known as the English Electric Type 4 and numbered D200 to D209, they were put to work and evaluated on the former Great Eastern line between London and Norwich, and on the East Coast Main Line. Initial reports among railwaymen and senior officials were unfavourable, who claimed that their performance was little better than that of a Britannia Class steam locomotive. However, the London Midland Region saw their potential as a replacement for their ageing express steam locomotives on routes that required good acceleration and sustained high speed, and this helped to secure a number of repeat orders. As with the Class 20s, developments in train-indicator systems at the time of production resulted in white discs being fitted to the earlier locomotives, and electric route-indicator boxes (of which there were several versions) to the later batches. From 1973, the class of 199 (one had been lost due to accident damage) became Class 40 under the TOPS classification system. Among enthusiasts the Class 40s gained the nickname 'Whistlers', due to the distinctive sound of their turbochargers. A Class 40, No. D326, was in charge of the mail train that was involved in the Great Train Robbery at Ledburn in Buckinghamshire, on 8 August 1963.

The introduction of more powerful diesel and electric traction in the 1970s meant that the Class 40s were soon relegated to secondary work, including heavy freight, which kept many active until the mid-1980s. The pioneer of the class, No. D200, was saved from scrapping by enthusiasts who managed to get the locomotive reinstated for use as a celebrity engine, and later secured as part of the National Collection.

263

SPECIFICATIONS

Class: 40
Power Type: Diesel-electric
First Built: 1958
Withdrawn: 1976–85
Builder: English Electric Co. & RSH Ltd
Number Built: 200

Wheel Arrangement: 1Co-Co1
Length: 69 ft 6 in
Weight: 136 tons
Max Speed: 90 mph
Liveries: BR (Green, Corporate Blue)
Names: Ocean liners (25)
Preserved: 7

CLASS 81

The first type of AC electric locomotive to enter service with British Railways was known as Class AL1 and under TOPS became Class 81. It formed one of five pioneer classes (AL1 to AL5), totalling one hundred locomotives, which were built by different manufacturers to evaluate designs for the development of future electric locomotives for use on the West Coast Main Line. Painted in a distinctive Electric Blue livery and capable of speeds of up to 100 mph, they were mixed-traffic machines based on a BR specification that was influenced by experience in France. These classes all had the same body shell, cab layouts, and pantographs. The latter collected 25 kV AC from overhead wires, and rectifiers were used to convert this into DC for powering the traction motors (initially equipped with two pantographs, only one was used in service and the other was removed to reduce maintenance). Due to the small clearances for the overhead wires under bridges and tunnels, the locomotives had to be capable of switching automatically to a lower voltage, but in practice this was not required due to improvements in the overhead infrastructure.

The AL1s entered traffic on the first section of the WCML to be electrified, between Manchester and Crewe, in September 1960. As electrification became more widespread they could be seen on all of the major WCML routes. On 6 January 1968, Class AL1 locomotive No. E3009 was hauling a passenger train which was in a fatal collision with a low-loader carrying a 120-ton transformer over a level crossing at Hixon in Staffordshire. The locomotive was destroyed and subsequently scrapped.

All of the early AC electric classes were prone to failures and fires, and were soon relegated to secondary duties such as parcels, freight, and empty stock. Although the first to be introduced and among the last to be withdrawn, the AL1s were not the most successful of the pioneer electric locomotive classes. This honour went to Class AL5 (Class 85), which underpinned the design for BR's first standard AC electric locomotive, the Class AL6 (Class 86).

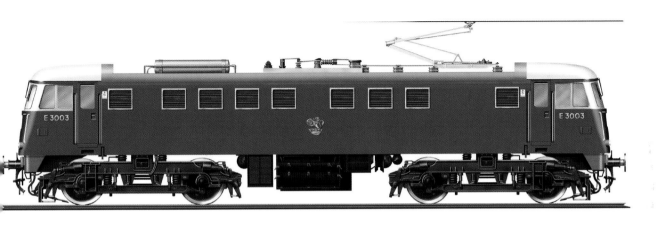

E3003

SPECIFICATIONS

Class: 81 (AL1)
Power Type: Electric (25 kV AC overhead)
First Built: 1959
Withdrawn: First 1968 (accident damage); Last 1992
Builder: BRC&W
Number Built: 25

Wheel Arrangement: Bo-Bo
Length: 56 ft 6 in
Weight: 80 tons
Max Speed: 100 mph
Liveries: BR (Electric Blue, corporate Blue)
Preserved: 1

CLASS 37

Under the Modernisation Plan for British Railways, the requirement for a versatile mixed-traffic diesel locomotive was identified. The English Electric Co. came forward with a design based on one that had been used for export to meet this requirement. It was known initially as the English Electric Type 3 and later as Class 37. Powered by a 1,750-hp English Electric 12CSVT engine and six traction motors, it bore a strong family resemblance to the English Electric Type 4 (Class 40), but was more compact and had a Co-Co wheel arrangement. Some were built with boilers for steam heating while on passenger duties.

Introduced in 1960, the class was an immediate success due to its excellent performance and reliability. The first examples saw service on the Eastern Region, with many operating passenger services in East Anglia, while others were employed on freight duties in the north east. From 1963 onwards, a considerable number were delivered to the Western Region for freight duties to and from the Welsh valleys. Eventually, Class 37s could be found the length and breadth of Great Britain, and were ideally suited to the Highland routes in Scotland. Among enthusiasts the class gained the nicknames 'Tractors' and 'Growlers', due to the agricultural sound of their exhaust.

During the mid-1980s, financial restraints meant that funding could not be provided to replace the diesel classes that had been in service since the late 1950s to the early 1960s. A major refurbishing programme was therefore embarked upon, which included a number of Class 37s. Specific modifications included replacement bogies and alternators, slow speed control, and electric train heating (ETH). Six locomotives were rebuilt to evaluate Mirrlees and Ruston engines. Due to the marked differences that resulted between individual locomotives and their equipment, several sub-classes were formed. With a relatively low axle loading offering wide route availability, some of these veteran machines continue to provide valuable service on both passenger and freight duties throughout the country. They have also been very popular with preservationists.

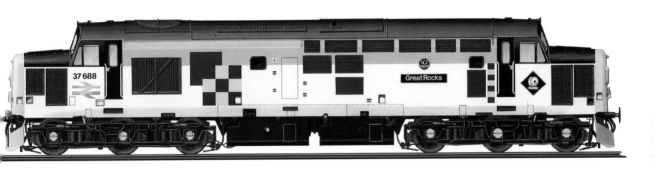

37688 *Great Rocks*

SPECIFICATIONS

Class: 37

Power Type: Diesel-electric

First Built: 1960

Withdrawn: Some still in service as at 2016

Builder: English Electric Co. & RSH Ltd

Number Built: 309

Wheel Arrangement: Co-Co

Length: 61 ft 6 in

Weight: 102–120 tons (varies by sub-class)

Max Speed: 80 mph

Liveries: BR (Green, Blue) Railfreight (various), numerous since privatisation

Preserved: 45 (as at 2016)

CLASS 55 'DELTIC'

n the mid-1950s, Britain's railways were facing stiff competition against the increasing use of motor vehicles and the expansion of the national motorway network. British Railway's modernisation plan was launched to counter this, and the replacement of steam with diesel traction gathered momentum. English Electric's prototype *Deltic* had proven capability, and the decision was taken to purchase a number of locomotives based on its design for use on the East Coast Main Line. The initial order was for twenty-three locomotives but this was reduced to twenty-two before the contract was signed. They cost £155,000 each, and were built over a two-year period at the English Electric Works at Newton-le-Willows.

When introduced in 1961, the Deltics were the most powerful diesel locomotives in the world, and could exceed 100 mph easily, with a fully laden train. Such was their efficiency that the twenty-two Deltics replaced fifty-five Gresley Class A3 and A4 Pacifics. They cut the London to Edinburgh time from eight hours to six, and this was improved further following upgrades to the route infrastructure. In the early 1970s they became known as Class 55, under British Rail's Total Operating Processing System (TOPS). During their short but hardworking careers the Deltics received modifications to make them compatible with the introduction of modern coaching stock. This included the replacement of vacuum brakes with air brakes, and the fitting of electric train-heating equipment. Prolonged high-speed running took its toll and the class was plagued by engine failures, but a pool of spare engines allowed a means of quick replacement and return to service.

The Deltics dominated ECML services until the introduction of the HST 125s in 1979. Some Deltics in need of heavy general overhauls were withdrawn as early as January 1980, while others soldiered on carrying out less demanding duties until the class was officially retired at the end of 1981. Six have been preserved, and some have ventured back onto the main line to haul charters and specials. One, surprisingly, has been hired out for freight duties.

D9009 *Alycidon*

SPECIFICATIONS

Class: 55 'Deltic'
Power Type: Diesel-electric
First Built: 1961
Withdrawn: 1980–82
Builder: English Electric Co.
Number Built: 22

Wheel Arrangement: Co-Co
Length: 69 ft 6 in
Weight: 100 tons
Max Speed: 105 mph
Liveries: BR (2-tone Green, Corporate Blue), Porterhouse Railways (Purple)
Names: Racehorses, Army regiments
Preserved: 6

CLASS 52 'WESTERN'

British Railway's Modernisation Plan of 1955 tended to favour the procurement of diesel locomotives with electric transmission but the Western Region opted for hydraulic transmission, due to its proven success on the West German railways (*Deutsche Bundesbahn*). In theory it offered reduced weight and thus a better power-to-weight ratio. Several designs were built, and some were more successful than others, such as the Class 42 Warship. However, none was powerful enough to take over the main line express duties from the King and Castle Class steam locomotives, so a higher performance machine was required. Building on previous experience, the Class 52, as it would become known, was born in 1961. It was powered by two MD655 engines (built under licence from Maybach), each rated at 1350-bhp with Voith hydraulic transmission to a pair of three-axle bogies. With its stylish and elegant appearance, it looked very different from any other British diesel design, and to add to their appeal, the class carried GWR-style cast number plates. All had names with 'Western' as a prefix, and hence they became known as the 'Westerns'. (Although officially Class 52 under TOPS, they never carried TOPS numbers.) Two locomotives were out-shopped in eye-catching experimental colours, No. D1000 in Desert Sand and No. D1015 in Golden Ochre.

The Class 52s were the most powerful diesel-hydraulic locomotive ever to be built in Great Britain. They were best known for their work on the premier express services between London and the west of England but were also highly capable of hauling heavy freight, including stone from the Foster Yeoman quarry at Merehead.

Unfortunately a number of factors came together that led to the Westerns' early demise – their lack of electric train-heating capability, an inability to operate in tandem and, ultimately, BR's decision to standardise with diesel-electric traction. First withdrawals began in 1973, and all were out of service by February 1977. Happily, the class enjoyed a strong following among enthusiasts, and seven were secured for preservation.

D1000 *Western Enterprise*

SPECIFICATIONS

Class: 52 'Western'
Power Type: Diesel-hydraulic
First Built: 1961
Withdrawn: 1973–7
Builder: BR (Crewe & Swindon)
Number Built: 74

Wheel Arrangement: C-C
Length: 68 ft
Weight: 108 tons
Max Speed: 90 mph
Liveries: BR (Maroon, Green, Blue, Desert Sand (1), Golden Ochre (1))
Names: Royal, regimental, and heraldic names prefixed by 'Western'
Preserved: 7 (including 1 in National Collection)

CLASS 47

British Railways' aim to eliminate its entire fleet of steam locomotives by 1968 placed tremendous pressure on the re-equipment programme. By 1962, many steam locomotives had already been scrapped, while a number of the first-generation diesels were proving troublesome or failed to meet expectations. There was an urgent need for a large number of mixed-traffic diesels with a power output of at least 2,500 hp and a low axle loading. To examine this requirement, three prototype locomotives were built by competing firms. However, due to time constraints they were not fully evaluated, and a contract was awarded to Brush Traction to build a new class of locomotive, incorporating an up-rated version of the Sulzer power unit that had been fitted to one of the prototypes (No. D0280 *Lion*). The result was the Brush Type 4, which under TOPS became Class 47.

Before the first example was delivered in 1962, there was sufficient confidence in the design to order a further thirty locomotives. Over the next six years, several more batches were built, which brought the total to 512, making it the largest class of mainline diesel in BR history. Differences in train-heating capability resulted in sub-classes being formed, and those without train heating were intended mainly for freight duties. In the late 1960s, the engines were de-rated from 2,750 hp to 2,580 hp, in order to reduce mechanical stress and improve reliability. One locomotive (No. D1628) was badly damaged in an accident and was rebuilt as a test-bed for Ruston engines. Over the years a number of other modifications were incorporated, including push-pull equipment, slow speed control, and long-range fuel tanks, the latter making them ideally suited for cross-country services. Thirty-three locomotives were rebuilt with Electro-Motive Diesel engines and reclassified as Class 57.

The decline in locomotive-hauled passenger services and the introduction of modern freight locomotives led to the gradual withdrawal of the class from the early 1990s onwards. Now around fifty years old, a few remain in service on the main line, and several have been preserved for use on heritage railways.

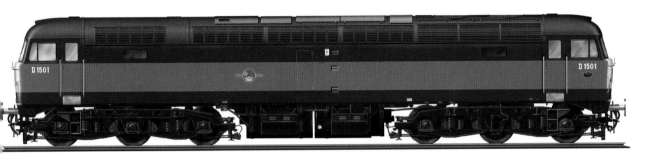

D1501

SPECIFICATIONS

Class: 47
Power Type: Diesel-electric
First Built: 1962
Withdrawn: From 1986 – some still in service
Builder: Brush Traction Ltd & BR Crewe
Number Built: 512
Wheel Arrangement: Co-Co

Length: 63 ft 6 in
Weight: 111–125 tons (varies by sub-class)
Max Speed: 95 mph (Class 47/7 – 100 mph)
Liveries: BR (2-tone Green, Blue), Railfreight, numerous private and celebrity liveries
Names: Initially only on Western Region locos; various names applied in later years
Preserved: 37 (as at 2016)

CLASS 50

One of the three prototypes that was built for evaluation by British Railways to meet the requirement for a diesel locomotive with a power output of at least 2,500 hp was known as DP2. Built by English Electric, its appearance resembled a production Deltic (Class 55) but internally it was a totally different machine. BR was attracted by the performance of its English Electric 16CSVT 2,700-hp engine, and placed an order for fifty, albeit incorporating a number of their own design requirements. Due to BR's financial problems at the time, the locomotives were leased initially for a ten-year period with English Electric's own engineers providing maintenance at depots. They were known as the second-generation English Electric Type 4 and became Class 50 under TOPS.

All of the class entered service between 1967 and 1968 on the West Coast Main Line, primarily for top-link express services between Crewe and Glasgow. They often operated in tandem, producing superb performances on this steeply graded route. When electrification of the WCML was completed in 1974, the entire class was transferred to the Western Region to replace the fleet of Class 52 diesel-hydraulics that were being withdrawn. Unfortunately, due to their prolonged high-speed running, the locomotives became run down, and a decision was taken to conduct a major refurbishment programme. This work was undertaken by BR's Doncaster Works between 1979 and 1984. After returning to service, their reliability and availability improved considerably. A distinctive feature of the refurbished locomotives was the addition of a high-intensity headlight at each end. The class was nicknamed 'Hoovers' by enthusiasts, due to the distinctive sound made by their cooling fans.

Although the Class 50s were displaced by High Speed Trains (Class 43), they soldiered on with less demanding duties. One locomotive was modified, unsuccessfully, to examine the class's potential as heavy freight engines. The majority of the class were retired in the early 1990s but, due to their popularity, three 'celebrities' were retained for rail tours until 1994, and many have been preserved.

50046 *Ajax*

SPECIFICATIONS

Class: 50
Power Type: Diesel-electric
First Built: 1967
Withdrawn: 1987–94
Builder: English Electric Co.
Number Built: 50

Wheel Arrangement: Co-Co
Length: 68 ft 6 in
Weight: 117 tons
Max Speed: 100 mph
Liveries: BR (Blue, Large Logo), GWR (Green*), NSE, Railfreight (1), civil engineers (1), various in preservation
Names: Famous warships, *Sir Edward Elgar**
Preserved: 18

CLASS 43 HIGH SPEED TRAIN

By the early 1970s, British Rail was facing stiff competition from the increasing popularity of the motor car. To overcome this it needed to offer a reliable alternative that offered speed and comfort for business commuters and long-distance travellers. The long-term aim was for widespread electrification but due to financial restraints, this would take time. It was therefore decided to develop a new concept in high-speed diesel trains, whereby a locomotive would be attached to each end of a fixed rake of modern, air-conditioned coaches. A prototype was built and tested between 1973 and 1976, by which time BR was convinced of its potential. Production orders were placed and the locomotives (known as power cars) were built at Crewe while the coaching stock was built at Derby. The locomotives were powered by a lightweight, 12-cylinder Paxman Valenta 2,250-hp engine and four Brush traction motors (a few were fitted with GEC traction motors). With its aerodynamic nose and lack of buffers, the external appearance gave an impression of style and speed. They became known as Class 43 and the sets as High Speed Trains (HSTs). In service they were branded the Inter-City 125, as they were capable of sustaining 125 mph on certain sections of track. The presence of a locomotive at each end of the train allowed rapid turnarounds at termini, while offering continued operation en route, should one unit develop a problem.

First introduced on the Western Region and later the East Coast Main Line, the HSTs revolutionised passenger services. On some timetables, HSTs were scheduled with a start-to-stop time requiring an average speed of over 100 mph, the first time this had occurred in the history of British railways. Other principal routes that subsequently adopted HSTs included the Midland Main Line and Cross-Country services. In 1987, an HST set a new world record for diesel traction of 148.3 mph.

Since 2005 the Class 43s have been re-engined to improve efficiency and, often dubbed 'the best trains ever built in Britain', this will ensure that the HSTs will be around for some time to come.

43002 *Sir Kenneth Grange*

SPECIFICATIONS

Class: 43
Power Type: Diesel-electric
First Built: 1975
Withdrawn: 3 due to accident damage
Builder: BR Crewe
Number Built: 197

Wheel Arrangement: Bo-Bo
Length: 58 ft 5 in
Weight: 70 tons
Max Speed: 125 mph
Liveries: BR (Blue/Grey, Inter-City), numerous liveries since privatisation
Names: Various names applied over the years, relevant to routes, people, and events
Preserved: 0 (as at 2016)

CLASS 90

I n the late 1980s, British Rail introduced a fleet of mixed-traffic electric locomotives known as Class 90. The design was based on experience from earlier electric types, and incorporated many state-of-the-art features including rheostatic brakes (in addition to air brakes), microprocessors to detect motor slipping, thyristor control for smooth acceleration, and Time Division Multiplexer (TDM) equipment to allow multiple and push-pull working. The first machine was out-shopped from Crewe Works in 1987 wearing the Inter-City Swallow livery that had been introduced to symbolise grace and speed. The Class 90s are powered by four GEC Alstholm traction motors that produce 5,000 hp. Capable of 110-mph running, they entered service on the West Coast Main Line and later on the East Coast Main Line, where they often deputised for Class 91s. In May 1988, a brand new member of the class (No. 90008) was shipped to the Continent and displayed at the Hamburg International Transport Traffic Exhibition along with two other British electric locomotives.

The Class 90s are, perhaps, the most colourful class of locomotives ever to operate on Britain's railways, having worn no fewer than twenty-seven different liveries in their thirty-year history. From the outset, many Class 90s were dedicated freight locomotives, and were identifiable by their attractive three-tone Railfreight Distribution livery. In 1991, five locomotives were repainted in Rail Express Systems livery (as illustrated) and were employed on dedicated postal trains between London, the Midlands, and the North. The following year, three locomotives were painted in pseudo-European Railways' liveries (Belgian, German, and French) and were all named *Freight Connection* in the appropriate European language.

Upon the privatisation of British Rail in 1996, the Class 90 fleet was divided between several operators including Virgin Trains, DB Schenker, and Freightliner. In 2004, fifteen Class 90s were transferred to the Great Eastern Main Line, where they are still active under the control of the current operator – Abellio Greater Anglia.

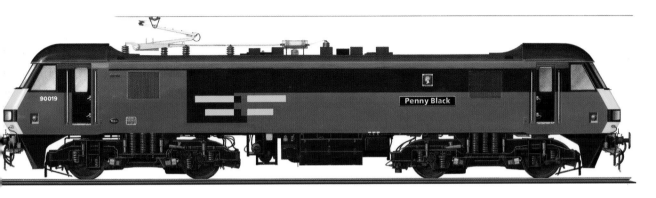

90019 *Penny Black*

SPECIFICATIONS

Class: 90
Power Type: Electric (25 kV AC overhead)
First Built: 1987
Withdrawn: 1 (90050 – fire damage); a few in store (as at 2016)
Builder: BREL Crewe Works
Number Built: 50

Wheel Arrangement: Bo-Bo
Length: 61 ft 6 in
Weight: 84.5 tons
Max Speed: 110 mph
Liveries: BR (Intercity, Mainline, RfD), GNER, One, NXEA, DBS, AGA, DRS, Freightliner, RES, EWS, FScR, VT, and others.
Names: Prominent figures and institutions, freight connections, and some individual names

CLASS 91

Electrification of the East Coast Main Line during the late 1980s offered significant improvements in the speed and frequency of trains on this historic route. More importantly, it reduced operating costs significantly when compared to diesel traction. To equip the new services, British Rail developed a train known as the Inter-City 225, which was capable of 140 mph (225 km/h). The concept was to have an electric locomotive coupled to a rake of modern Mark 4 coaches, with an unpowered Driving Van Trailer (DVT) at the other end, to provide a push-pull capability.

GEC won the contract to design and build the locomotives. They produced an unusual design, which they called Project Electra, in that the locomotive had a streamlined end and a blunt end. The streamlined end reduced drag during high-speed running, while the blunt end blended with the leading coach to reduce turbulence on the pantograph. The locomotives, known as Class 91, could be driven from either end, albeit rarely from the blunt end. The traction motors, which, unusually, are mounted in the body, could develop 6,300 hp, making it the most powerful passenger locomotive ever built in Britain.

Sadly the true potential of the Inter-City 225 was never realised, due to the speed restrictions imposed by incompatible signalling. However, a few short sections of the ECML were upgraded for proving tests, which resulted in some record-breaking runs. On 17 September 1989 a Class 91 (No. 91010) attained a speed of 161.7 mph, which remains a record for a British locomotive. Another member of the class (No. 91032) achieved the fastest ever time between Kings Cross and Edinburgh, at just under three and a half hours, and an average speed of 112.5 mph.

Prolonged high-speed running on an intensive timetable eventually took its toll on reliability, and the entire fleet of Class 91s had to be put through a refurbishment programme between 2000 and 2003. Along with upgraded coaches, this ensured that the Inter-City 225 would remain the flagship of the ECML until the introduction of Hitachi Class 800 units.

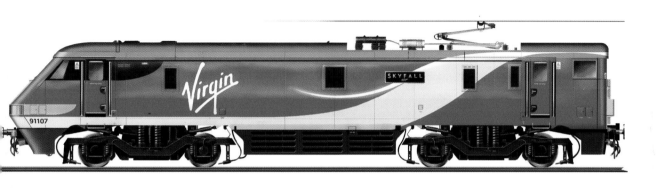

91107 *Skyfall*

SPECIFICATIONS

Class: 91
Power Type: Electric (25 kV AC overhead)
First Built: 1988
Builder: BREL Crewe Works
Number Built: 31
Refurbished: 2000–3

Withdrawn: None (as at 2016)
Wheel Arrangement: Bo-Bo
Length: 63 ft 7¾ in
Weight: 81.5 tons
Max Speed: 140 mph (110 mph blunt end first)
Liveries: BR (Intercity), GNER, NXEC (1), East Coast, Virgin Trains East Coast
Names: Various, including local themes, personalities, special events, military connections, promotional (temporary)

CLASS 66

When British Rail's freight operations were privatised in 1996, a new company was formed, called the English Wales & Scottish (EWS) Railway. It took control of approximately 93 per cent of the UK's rail freight business, and a fleet of ageing diesel locomotives that were expensive to operate and maintain. At the time, the Foster Yeoman company was operating privately owned American-built diesel locomotives for hauling aggregate from their quarries in Somerset over BR tracks. The performance of these locomotives, known as Class 59, was superb, and their reliability was exceptional. EWS was so impressed by them that it placed an order for two hundred and fifty similar machines, known as Class 66, which were built at the Electro-Motive Diesel (EMD) plant in Canada. Power was provided by the well-proven 12-cylinder EMD710 3,300-hp engine with six General Motors traction motors, which differed from the Class 59, to enable higher speeds. Other key features included an 1,800-gallon fuel tank which, being over twice the capacity of a Class 47, offered long range and increased availability, and radial steering bogies to reduce track wear.

The introduction of Class 66 locomotives represented a radical shift in British locomotive policy towards procurement from overseas suppliers. These superb locomotives reinvigorated the rail freight business at a time when it needed to be more efficient and competitive. Such was their success that subsequent orders were placed by Freightliner, GB Railfreight, and Direct Rail Services. The class have operated all over the British network and, in addition to freight, their duties have included engineering and works trains, nuclear flask trains, and the occasional passenger charter. The class inherited the nickname 'Sheds' by enthusiasts, due to their front-end profile and angular roof.

The introduction of stringent emission regulations has meant that it is unlikely that any more new Class 66 locomotives will be ordered. However, a considerable number of locomotives, known as the EMD Series 66, have been purchased by European railway companies, and a few of these have been imported for conversion to UK specifications.

66200 *Railway Heritage Committee*

SPECIFICATIONS

Class: 66
Power Type: Diesel-electric
First Built: 1998
Withdrawn: 2 (due to accident damage)
Builder: Electric-Motive Diesel (Canada)
Number Built: 446

Wheel Arrangement: Co-Co
Length: 70 ft 3 in
Weight: 129.6 tons
Max Speed: 75 mph (Class 66/6 – 65 mph)
Liveries: EWS, GBRf, Freightliner, DRS, DBS, Colas, Eddie Stobart, and various others
Names: A few have individual names, including football teams and heritage railways (mainly Class 66/7)

CLASS 68

Class 68 is a fleet of mixed-traffic diesel locomotives that are used to haul both passenger and freight trains. A significant advantage of their design is a combination of low axle loading, high power output and high speed. The locomotives are built by Vossloh in Spain and, at the time of writing, thirty-two have been ordered. The locomotive is powered by a sixteen-cylinder, 3,800-hp engine supplied by Caterpillar Inc. The first locomotive, No. 68001, spent several months during 2013 at the Velim Test Centre in the Czech Republic prior to delivery. The second locomotive, No. 68002, was the first to arrive in the United Kingdom in January 2014.

The fleet of Class 68 locomotives are owned by Direct Rail Services but six have been leased to Chiltern Railways for use on their main line services. These are fitted with push-pull equipment to allow them to operate with Mark III coaches and a Driving Van Trailer (DVT), which negates the need to uncouple the locomotive for return journeys. ScotRail also operate two leased Class 68s on services from Edinburgh on the Fife Circle Line. Looking to the future, it is planned that seven Class 68s will be leased from DRS for use on TransPennine Express services.

As the most modern diesel locomotive currently operating on Britain's railways, the Class 68's versatility and efficiency is likely to ensure that they will provide reliable service for many years to come.

The Class 88 is a recent development of the Class 68. These locomotives feature the same body shell, cab, bogies, traction equipment and control software as the Class 68 but are dual mode, capable of operating from either 25kV AC overhead line equipment or by an internal diesel engine. As such, the Class 88 will be the first dual mode locomotive to use the overhead system on the British railway network as the only other electro-diesels draw current from the 750 V DC 3rd rail system used by the Southern Region. At the time of writing, DRS had ordered ten Class 88s to serve as mixed traffic locomotives on routes that are not fully electrified.

68009 *Titan*

SPECIFICATIONS

Class: 68
Power Type: Diesel-electric
First Built: 2013
Withdrawn: None (as at 2016)
Builder: Vossloh (Spain)
Number Built: 32 (as at 2016)

Wheel Arrangement: Bo-Bo
Length: 66 ft 8 in
Weight: 85 tons
Max Speed: 100 mph
Liveries: DRS, ScotRail, Chiltern Railways
Names: Some named after warships

ABBREVIATIONS AND DEFINITIONS

AC: Alternating Current

Auto-coach: A type of coach used in push-pull trains, with a driving cab at one end and a locomotive at the other

BR: British Railways or British Rail (post-1965)

BREL: British Rail Engineering Limited

CR: Caledonian Railway

DBS: Deutsche Bahn Schenker

DC: Direct Current

DRS: Direct Rail Services

DVT: Driving Van Trailer

ECML: East Coast Main Line

ETH: Electric Train Heating

EWS: English Wales & Scottish Railway

FScR: First Scot Rail

GBRf: GB Railfreight

GCR: Great Central Railway

GNER: Great North Eastern Railway

GNR: Great Northern Railway

GNSR: Great North of Scotland Railway

GWR: Great Western Railway

HST: High Speed Train

kV: 1000 Volts

LBSCR: London Brighton & South Coast Railway

LMS: London Midland & Scottish Railway

LNER: London & North Eastern Railway

LSWR: London & South Western Railway

MR: Midland Railway

NBL: North British Locomotive Company

NBR: North British Railway

NER: North Eastern Railway

NXEA: National Express East Anglia

NXEC: National Express East Coast

RES: Rail Express Systems

RfD: Railfreight Distribution

RN: Royal Navy

RSH: Robert Stephenson & Hawthorns

SR: Southern Railway (or Southern Region)(BR)

Superheater: A device used to reheat steam in order to increase thermal efficiency

TOPS: Total Operations Processing System

VF: Vulcan Foundry

VT: Virgin Trains

WCML: West Coast Main Line

WD: War Department